2

THE BOX
OF
DAYLIGHT

TCHAMSEM QUICKLY PRESSED THE LID DOWN
WITH ALL HIS STRENGTH.

THE BOX
OF DAYLIGHT

by

WILLIAM HURD HILLYER

and with drawings by
ERICK BERRY

Junior Literary Guild   New York 1931

C O N T E N T S

CONTENTS

LIST OF ILLUSTRATIONS

THE BOX OF DAYLIGHT

Introduction

The stories contained in "The Box of Daylight" were begun in 1916. It was this year that the Government Printing office published the "31st Annual Report of the Bureau of American Ethnology to the Secretary of the Smithsonian Institute, for 1909–1910," which contained a study by Dr. Franz Boas on the "Tsimshian Mythology, based on the texts of Henry W. Tate." This work remains to date the outstanding and practically the only authority on the habits, culture and legends of this particular people of the Nass River valley.

The story itself is based on the myths of the Haida, Tlingit, and the Tsimshian tribes of British Columbia, on Prince Charlotte Island and the adjacent mainland.

These tribes have from time immemorial lived in wooden houses, and have used copper as a medium of exchange. They appear to be culturally and racially distinct from all the other so-called Indians of North America.

The report came to my notice soon after it was published. A copy had been sent to former Senator Hoke Smith, of Georgia, who, knowing my interest in lore of this sort, gave me the book.

Here I discovered the story of the Raven, which I recognized as one of the most fascinating and colorful of the legends of North America. I began to study the text carefully. As I read the confused and sometimes contradictory versions of the myths, the essentials of the story began to take form. Here was the universal pattern—a cosmology, story of creation and so on—but here also was a real hero, Indian style. Tchamsem—brave, strong, boastful, crafty, devoted, greedy, treacherous, successful—cried out for a biographer.

So "The Box of Daylight" began. The cycle of tales was not completed until the spring of 1924, when it was put into approximately its present form.

I have endeavored to reproduce the spirit of wonder and poetic simplicity which the old Indian narrators must have felt as they told the tales, and at the same time avoid the redundancies, inconsistencies, and contradictions of the myths in their verbatim form.

A word about Tchamsem's songs. These were in-
spired by the numerous songs and songlets in the text
with which the Indians embellished their narratives.

In several instances it has been necessary to diverge
from the spelling of proper names used in the scientific
work. The most notable of these is the spelling of
"Tchamsem" itself, which is written in Dr. Boas's paper,
"Txamsem," and which would be unpronounceable to
the average reader. The "x" in recording the Tsimshian
language, according to Dr. Boas, is used to indicate a
sound almost like the German "ch" in Bach. Since our
"ch" would come nearer than our "x" to approximating
the sound to the general reader, I have elected to use it
instead of the scientific spelling, although aware that it
fails to bring out the guttural qualities of the Indian
language.

Needless to say, the descriptions of customs, dress,
houses, villages, and amusements check with the authori-
ties down to the most minute detail.

William Hurd Hillyer
February, 1931

My grandfather sang me a conjuror's song:
He had one hundred conjuror's songs.
From his grandfather them he heard—
Big medicine in every word.
By light of smoldering red fires
He sang the exploits of his sires—
He of the crested raven clan—
Whose chief was neither bird nor man.
And of that chief (so old, so old,
Time out of mind it hath been told)
The conjurors have always sung
With roaring rattle and rhythmic tongue;
Because the daylight first, and then
Nine other gifts he gained for men—
Tchamsem the Raven, crafty, strong;
My grandfather sang me a conjuror's song.

THE BOX
OF
DAYLIGHT

THE BOX OF DAYLIGHT

PROLOGUE

In the very night of time lived only Anvik, the Oversky Chief, with his wife and three children. The two eldest were boys: one was named Walking-About-Early, and the other Climbing Cloud. The youngest was a girl, and her name was Kedilla, which means "Princess."

The earth was dark in those days, because Anvik kept all the daylight in a great round box behind the door of his house. Once a year he carried the box to the top of a high hill in the Oversky Country, where he let loose enough daylight for himself and his family, but no more. Only a very little found its way through the Hole-in-the-Sky to the dim Earth, where no people lived, only the Quelemos, the Web-footed Frogs, and their cousins, the Ghosts—who were not counted as living beings at all, but only lumps and shadows.

Anvik had three slaves, Old-Man-Who-Foresees-Trouble, He-Who-Knows-Everything-That-Happens, and Big-Sounding-Drumbelly, who were charged with the care of the box of daylight and who also guarded the Princess.

Now, Old-Man-Who-Foresees-Trouble had a dream in which he saw the god Raven come up through the Hole-in-the-Sky and steal the box of daylight from Anvik. He thereupon warned the chieftain, who scowled at his fears.

Climbing Cloud and Walking-About-Early were bitter rivals for the honor of carrying the box of daylight for their father. But Walking-About-Early was Anvik's favorite.

At that time there were no people on Earth—only, as we have said, lumps and shadows. But Stone and Elderberry could scarce be counted as such, for Stone was a very ancient god, more solid and steadfast than the croaking Frogs, and Elderberry was far less shadowy than the ghosts.

So Stone and Elderberry each resolved to create real People—beings who should have form and life and substance, with just the faintest resemblance to the gods. This was a difficult task, and both Stone and Elderberry labored mightily, each trying to create People first. And had Stone succeeded, the People would have been hard and cold and enduring, but would have lacked all sap and gladness, and there would have been no joy in them.

Now, of all the high gods the swiftest and cleverest was Raven, who was equally at home in the Oversky regions and on the dim Earth. And one day Raven, flying fast and far, beheld Stone and Elderberry each struggling to create People. Whereat he saw quickly that if Stone succeeded, the People would lack all sap and gladness—which was displeasing to the debonair Raven. So he called to Elderberry to push hard with his roots, and Elderberry pushed against Stone so hard and steadily that Stone rolled over on the People that he was creating, and they died there. So Elderberry created People without hindrance, and their sap and gladness were pleasing to Raven, though he bemoaned their want of daylight. Scarce could they see to fish, so great was the darkness.

Raven grieved more and more for his People, because they had no daylight, save the very little that filtered through the Hole-in-the-Sky to the dark Earth.

So he resolved to steal the box of daylight from the Oversky Chief, that they might enjoy the gladness wherewith they were born.

Sometimes Anvik had let his daughter Kedilla carry the box in her arms, and after countless ages the luminous image of her face became imprinted on the lid. And when at length the first box was exhausted and Anvik obtained a fresh one from the high supernatural gods, he gave the old box to his daughter, and she carries it across the sky at night even to this day. And when folks see the luminous image of her face on the lid of the box, they say: "There goes Princess Moon."

The box of daylight that Raven resolved to steal was the second one, quite fresh, and closely packed with daylight by the high supernatural gods.

So Raven went through the Hole-in-the-Sky to steal the box of daylight from the Oversky Chief. And the first thing that he saw was the Princess Moon with the luminous lid in her arms. Her he pursued, for he had fallen madly in love. Kedilla ran from him over the rim of Ocean, and thence down through Ocean, coming back over the Great Mountain on the far edge of the Oversky Country; and all of her father's people welcomed her back with cheers.

Ever since that time it has been good luck to see the Moon over one's left shoulder, for that was how Anvik and Princess Moon's brothers saw her when she returned.

Very glad was everyone to see her, for Anvik let loose so little daylight from his box that even the Oversky Country was a place of twilight; and the luminous lid of the empty box which Princess Moon carried gave the celestial inhabitants enough light for their heavenly fishing.

(I) : Tchamsem is Born

Here begins the most amazing part of the whole history of Raven; wherein we see him outwitting celestial beings, triumphing over obstacles—almost defying the decrees of the high supernatural gods; which had he not done, we should have had no daylight, no fire, no fresh water, no halibut, no salmon; indeed, it is doubtful if we ourselves should have existed, you and I.

At the back of the chief's house in the Oversky Country was a spring, where the Princess used to drink. After the strange dream of her slave, Old-Man-Who-Foresees-Trouble, and especially after her escapade under the earth from ocean to mountains, she was more jealously guarded than ever; but in fine, clear weather she still on rare occasions went to the spring.

Now, Raven was possessed of two apparently conflicting emotions—love for the Princess and a burning resolve to get the daylight for his people. The more he thought about it, the more hopeless seemed his plight and the more vexed he became—until suddenly, as he watched from his hiding-place the Princess drinking at the spring, he hit upon a plan.

He saw plainly that in order to accomplish his purpose he must be born into the chief's own family and be brought up as his grandson—he must have the box of daylight for his plaything.

He must be not merely the Princess Moon's husband; he must be her son.

How he achieved this miracle by transforming himself into a hemlock leaf, which was swallowed by the Princess when she drank from the spring; and how she called her little son Tchamsem—is all poetry and is duly sung and chanted by a thousand magicians, to the accompaniment of their bull-roaring rattles.

So Tchamsem was born, and he grew up in the house of the Oversky Chief, who kept the box of daylight hanging behind his door.

(II) : Tchamsem Cries for the Mâa

Tchamsem grew with astounding rapidity. Soon his crib became too small for him, and his mother had to spread blankets for him on the floor. His grandfather, the Oversky Chief, picked the child up and turned him over and over and thumped him from head to foot, saying: "You young dog, how fat you are!"

And then he turned to the child's grandmother, and said: "Look at him! Not a flaw!"

Then he handed Tchamsem back to the Princess, but the child was so heavy that she could not hold him; so the chief laughed and put Tchamsem down on the blankets again.

"Ha!" he cried. "So your great prince is too big for you, eh? Great fat prince! Ha!"

All this time the Mâa, the round box of daylight, hung behind the door of the chief's house.

One day Tchamsem began to cry. His mother and his grandmother tried to comfort him. He cried louder than ever; he was saying something, but they could not make it out.

"Hamáxa! hamáxa!" cried Tchamsem. He sat up, and beat the floor with his two baby fists; yet so strong he was that the ground shook, and the two women looked at each other and trembled.

Just then the chief came in. For a moment his grandson stopped crying; then he burst forth louder than ever.

"Hamáxa! hamáxa! hamáxa!"

"What is he saying?" asked the child's mother.

"What is he saying?" asked his grandmother.

"Fools!" roared the chief. "Have you no ears? He is crying for the Mâa!"

"He is crying for the Mâa!" exclaimed the mother and grandmother, in one breath.

Then the chief, who was indeed a doting grandfather and could deny his grandson nothing whatsoever, reached up and took the Mâa, the round box in which daylight was kept, from its place behind the door, and gave it to Tchamsem to play with. And Tchamsem crowed for joy and crawled about with great glee, pushing and rolling the box of daylight all over the floor; the terrible Mâa was his plaything, for he was the grandson of the Oversky Chief.

(III) : More Trouble about the Mâa

When the time came for the Oversky Chief to take the Mâa out to the high hill and release enough daylight to last the rest of the year, his grandson Tchamsem, that lusty infant, was playing with it as usual—rolling it about on the floor and thumping it fiercely with his fists. Every now and then he would utter a strange cry, a sort of half-exultant shout:

"Ha! Ha!"

Sometimes it would sound like this:

"Haw! Haw!" And then: "Qaw! Qaw!"

"Listen at the child!" cried his grandmother. "You would almost think he were a raven!"

Whereat they all laughed—the two women and the chief; but the old slaves did not laugh, and Old-Man-Who-Foresees-Trouble remembered his dream.

"Master," he ventured, "great master—"

"Speak, slave!" snapped the chief, whirling upon him. "If you have aught to say, say it quickly; I lack patience with your long drivelings."

"Good master," said Old-Man-Who-Foresees-Trouble, "are you sure it is quite safe for His Highness the Prince to play with the terrible Mâa?"

"Safe—safe?" echoed the chief. "In what way? For the Prince or for the box?"

"For either," returned the slave quietly. "As your lordship knows, the daylight is packed in the box very tightly. Very great indeed the pressure by which it seeks to escape. And even your lordship, when he carries the Mâa to the top of the hill once a year, must needs be very cautious and skillful when he lifts the lid ever so little, lest the daylight rush out all at once and burn up the world. Now, His Highness the Prince—"

"Hold your tongue!" commanded the chief. "The box is very strong. The lid is firmly fastened. The Prince is my grandson. He shall have what he wants."

"But your lordship," the slave began again. "The high supernatural gods—"

"Begone!" thundered his master. "Begone from my sight! Another word, and I will have your lying old tongue cut out like a cormorant's!"

Whereupon the aged slave withdrew; but his heart was sad within him.

Then the Oversky Chief told Tchamsem's mother to take the Mâa away from the child and bring it to him so that he could carry it out to the top of the high hill and let loose the year's supply of daylight.

But when she approached Tchamsem and tried to take the Mâa, he held it yet tighter and began to weep. And she could not take it from him.

Neither could his grandmother take the box away from Tchamsem.

So his grandfather, Anvik the Oversky Chief himself, came forward, and he took the box of daylight from his infant grandson; but the noise, the weeping, the yelling, the thwacking, the kicking of infant heels, and the pounding of huge pudgy fists were things to be remembered, even in heaven.

(IV) : Boyhood of Tchamsem

Year after year the same thing occurred, for the Mâa was Tchamsem's constant plaything: the chief would take the box away from his grandson (after the mother and the grandmother had failed to do so) and carry it up to the top of the high hill to release a year's supply of daylight. And each time there was a greater struggle —a louder noise, more profuse weeping, and yet more frightful yelling and thwacking and kicking, and beating of boyish fists, than before. For Tchamsem was

17

indeed becoming a young giant; but the chief was proud
of his overgrown grandson and called him "Giant" as a
nickname.

Now, one year when Anvik went to take the box of
daylight from Tchamsem, the chief looked, and behold!
the boy did not have it at all: he had gone and hung it
up in its accustomed place behind the door of the house.
And the chief was astonished. He looked at his grandson and saw him sitting very quietly, regarding Anvik
with a sober, shrewd expression. And the thought came
to the chief that here was a child no longer, not even a
boy, but a young man that was sitting there looking at
him. Almost did Anvik ask permission of his own grandson to take the box of daylight from its place behind the
door, where it was wont to hang before the high supernatural gods invented time. But he recollected himself
and went and took the box without a word; whereat
Tchamsem spoke up and said:

"Grandfather, may I go with you and hold the Mâa
while you unloosen the lid?"

Anvik thought for a moment; then he answered:

"Yes, you may go."

So Tchamsem went with his grandfather and held the
box of daylight on the high hill; this he did that year,
and the next. And the chief was very proud of his grandson's exploits, and he called him Giant.

(V) : The Three Slaves Warn Anvik

One day, early the next spring, Tchamsem said to his grandfather, Anvik:

"Grandfather, I have a great favor to ask."

Now, Tchamsem had never spoken quite in this wise before: he had for some years been quiet and respectful in his demeanor, but he had never spoken in this wise.

So Anvik listened, for he was proud of the young man; and he said:

"Whatever it be, ask it."

"Grandfather," returned Tchamsem, "let me take the Mâa, the box of daylight, all by myself this year and release the daylight from the high hill."

The Oversky Chief looked at his grandson, and for a long time he said nothing. At last he replied, very slowly:

"Not this year. Next year you may do what you ask."

But Old-Man-Who-Foresees-Trouble and He-Who-Knows-Everything-That-Happens and the third great slave, Big-Sounding-Drumbelly, held counsel together; and they waited on the chief, all three of them. And Old-Man-Who-Foresees-Trouble said:

"Great master, do but listen to thy poor slaves just this once and we shall be forever silent. Neither this year nor the next, we pray thee, permit His Highness the Prince to take the Mâa, the box of daylight, to the high hill. For behold, we are troubled in our sleep, and our dreams are all of the young man and the round box that hangs behind the door; and we see only danger."

And He-Who-Knows-Everything-That-Happens opened his mouth and spake after this wise:

"O master, we know that thou art Oversky Chief, and thy wisdom is above all wisdom, and thy power above all power, save only that of the high supernatural gods themselves. But we, thy poor slaves, whom these same gods have cursed with visions and with strange dreams, we see great danger and disaster unspeakable; and it is all by reason of the young Prince and the Mâa, the round box in which daylight is kept."

And Big-Sounding-Drumbelly, whose words were few and ill-chosen, but whose loyalty was matched only by his size and strength, nodded assent and pounded fiercely on his stomach.

Now the Oversky Chief, when his slaves had left off speaking, was silent for a long time. He did not voice his displeasure in loud and angry tones when at length he opened his mouth, but his words were all the more terrible because of their cool restraint.

"Slaves," he began, "ye are old. And because ye are old, your dreams are troubled, and your speech is wandering, and your actions exceeding childish. And again, because of your years and of your faithful service hitherto, I am inclined to spare you. But provoke me not further with your insolence, and blaspheme the gods not again, lest I destroy you utterly. I am old without age, and strong without brute strength; I need not slaves for counsel, nor fat men for power. The young Prince is my grandson. He goes alone to the high hill with the box of daylight next year, even as his grandfather before him has gone, ever since the high supernatural gods made heaven and earth. I have spoken."

And his two sons—Tchamsem's uncles—heard what Anvik had said to the three slaves; and they held their peace, for they feared the chief exceedingly. Nevertheless, they were ill content and murmured amongst themselves.

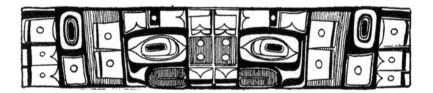

(VI): Tchamsem Steals the Box of Daylight

So the next year it came about that Tchamsem was intrusted with the Mâa, the box in which daylight is kept, kissed his mother and grandmother, and started off for the high hill. Before him to the east went Walking-About-Early, ready to snatch the box away from Tchamsem as soon as he should reach the high hill; and to the west went Climbing Cloud, as was his wont.

But the three slaves, Old-Man-Who-Foresees-Trouble and He-Who-Knows-Everything-That-Happens and Big-Sounding-Drumbelly, hid themselves in the deep woods behind the chief's house, and when Tchamsem came forth, bearing the great round box of daylight under his arm, these three slaves crept forward and followed him. And it was very dark, for there had been no daylight let loose for a whole year.

Now Tchamsem started in the direction of the high hill, as if to release a year's supply of daylight. But when he had gone a space, he turned and went towards the Hole-in-the-Sky, whence as Raven he had first come to the Oversky Country.

Dark as it was, He-Who-Knows-Everything-That-Happens saw Tchamsem turn aside from the path that led to the high hill, and he whispered to Big-Sounding-Drumbelly:

"See the Prince: he is going the wrong way!"

And Drumbelly, breathing hard in his excitement, whispered to Old-Man-Who-Foresees-Trouble:

"He is going the wrong way!"

The old slave stood still, and again he remembered his dream.

Then he looked; and behold, there was Tchamsem making off with the box of daylight in the direction of the Hole-in-the-Sky. The old slave sprang forward, but as he did so, the bushes crackled and Tchamsem began to run.

"He is running away with the Mâa!" muttered Old-Man-Who-Foresees-Trouble.

"He is running away with the Mâa!" cried the second old slave, He-Who-Knows-Everything-That-Happens.

Whereat Big-Sounding-Drumbelly beat a horrible tattoo on his stomach and yelled in a voice that woke all the echoes of heaven:

"The Mâa! the Mâa! He is running away with the Mâa!"

(VII) : Pursuit of Tchamsem

The Oversky Chief was sitting in his house, staring into the fire, and thinking what a fine grandson he had. When he heard the alarm raised by the three slaves, he sat up and listened, for he thought he must have been dreaming. And again the voice of Big-Sounding-Drumbelly and the other two slaves came echoing and re-echoing through the darkness:

"Hai! hai! The Mâa! the Mâa! Look at the Giant! He is running away with the Mâa!"

Then Anvik, the Oversky Chief, raised himself to his full height; and he took down his trusty bow, Sapdel, whose arrows were poisoned with all the sorrows of Time, and started in pursuit. Soon he overtook the three slaves, Old-Man-Who-Foresees-Trouble and He-Who-Knows-Everything-That-Happens and Big-Sounding-Drumbelly, and they all ran after Tchamsem; and all heaven was filled with their clamor.

Then it was that the good bird Ginsâa, to whom Raven had intrusted his blanket, suddenly appeared and returned the blanket to Tchamsem; it was big medicine.

Tchamsem quickened his pace and sought to elude his pursuers by plunging into the deepest thicket; but as he ran with the box of daylight, the lid became loosened and a little of the daylight leaked out and spilled on the ground like dazzling milk. So Anvik and his slaves took up the trail, and they followed him easily by reason of the leaking daylight.

From the east came Walking-About-Early, and from the west came Climbing Cloud. And they closed in upon their nephew, lighting their masks of pitch-wood meanwhile, so that the other pursuers could see their way more clearly.

Through the thickest woods, where the underbrush had not been disturbed since the high supernatural gods had their dream of creation, crashed the young giant Tchamsem, the three slaves and his two uncles and the

Oversky Chief close at his heels. He held the great box under his arm, and he wrapped his raven blanket tightly around him. But the faster he ran, the more daylight leaked out, until it poured forth in long, brilliant streamers and lit up the dark places of the forest.

So they came at length to the wide-open space in the midst of which is the village of Kungelas, where the celestial animals live; and beyond that is the Hole-in-the-Sky.

The Dog, the Porcupine, the Wolf, the Bear, and all the other animals awoke and heard the shouting and the thunderous tattoo of Big-Sounding-Drumbelly; and they saw the glare from the daylight that leaked forth from the Mâa as Tchamsem carried it. And they all came out and joined in the chase, and their own voices mingled with the shouts of the three slaves and the two uncles and with the terrible war-cry of the Oversky Chief.

But Tchamsem spread his raven blanket to the wind, and the wind bore him along more swiftly than his pursuers. And as he neared the Hole-in-the-Sky, Anvik and his two sons and the three slaves and all the celestial animals fetched forth a yell that shook the world and caused the high supernatural gods to stir uneasily in their seats.

And Tchamsem paused at the Hole-in-the-Sky and looked back for the first time and flung this defiance over his shoulder:

BUT TCHAMSEM SPREAD HIS RAVEN BLANKET
TO THE WIND, AND THE WIND BORE HIM ALONG
MORE SWIFTLY THAN HIS PURSUERS.

"Hai! hai! Come on, ye cowards! I am Tchamsem! I am the Raven! I am swifter and craftier than ye all, and I shall take the daylight to my people!"

Then Anvik, the Oversky Chief, stood still and fitted a poisoned arrow into his huge bow, Sapdel; and he took fair aim at Tchamsem.

"Great thief!" he cried. "Thus perish the foes of Anvik!"

And he let fly an arrow, poisoned with all the sorrows of Time, straight at Tchamsem just as the young man plunged through the Hole-in-the-Sky with the box of daylight; and the arrow missed him by a hair's breadth. But a drop of the poison fell upon Tchamsem's throat, and that is why the voice of the Raven is hoarse and full of sorrow, even to this day.

(VIII): Raven Returns to His People

Through the Hole-in-the-Sky went Tchamsem, carrying under his arm the Mâa, the box in which daylight is kept; and his raven blanket became as wings and held him so that he fell but ever so gently.

Now, there are many villages between the earth and the sky; we see the smoke from their houses and we say: "Look at the clouds, they are just like smoke." And at the first village a Person came out to meet Tchamsem. This

Person had a torch, for it was very dark, in spite of the daylight that leaked out from the Mâa; and he handed the torch to Tchamsem. But Tchamsem flew so fast that the torch went out, and he threw it down to earth. So it was at all the villages. And there were twice as many of these burnt torches on earth as before; there they are at the mouth of Nass River to this day.

At length came Tchamsem to his own domain, the country of the Raven clan. He had wrapped his raven blanket about him and now he was Raven indeed, he who had left the earth so long ago to get daylight for his people. But a new generation had arisen since Raven started on his quest, and none of the people knew him. They were in great misery, for our friends the Frogs (some of whom had survived when Stone rolled over them) had made common cause with the Ghosts; and while the Frogs, those clever fishermen, stole all the good fishing, the Ghosts came and stole the sleep from the eyes of men. So it had come to pass that men could neither eat nor sleep. Many had perished, and there remained only a handful, near the mouth of the River Nass, where Tchamsem landed.

"Qa ! qa !" cried Tchamsem. "Miserable creatures that ye are, have ye no courage, no manhood, that ye permit the Frogs (who are only lumps) to steal your good fishing, and the Ghosts (who after all are but shadows) to pilfer the very sleep from your eyes?"

"It is even so," replied the headman of the village. "But what can we do? The Frogs are stronger than we, being first cousins of the steadfast Rocks; and the Ghosts are cleverer, having lived so many lives already that they care not to live again in the flesh. They thrive upon

darkness; and behold, we have no daylight; so what can we do?"

"Give me food," said Tchamsem.

"Alas, chief," answered the headman—for he respected the raven blanket—"alas, we have only a few dried herrings, for the Frogs have stolen all the halibut and the salmon; but to such as we have you are welcome." And he gave him the dried herrings.

"Give me fresh water," commanded Tchamsem.

In like manner the headman of the village bewailed

the lack of fresh water; the water which they had was only brackish.

"I am cold," said Tchamsem. "Build me a warm fire."

"Alas, most worthy chief," replied the headman, "we are in sad case indeed, for we know that there is such a thing as fire, for the stars have it and now and then one of their burning torches falls to earth; but, as for us, we burrow in the ground for the winter and we eat our food raw."

Then the Prince looked long and earnestly at his people—his own people of the Raven clan—and he lifted up his head and flung back his dark blanket.

"Fear not, O people of mine," he declaimed in a loud voice. "I am Tchamsem, the Raven; and I bring you daylight, even the daylight of the high supernatural gods!"

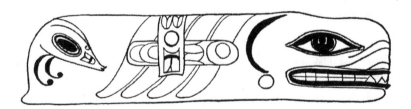

(IX) : He Opens the Box of Daylight

Tchamsem went westward; and behold, the Frogs were gathered in great numbers on the river's edge, ready to take away all the good fishing. And on the river were the Ghosts, ready to steal the sleep from the eyes of men. Tchamsem could not see the Ghosts, but he heard them gibbering and whistling in the dark, and now and then he caught the *swish swish* of their spectral canoes.

And he watched how the Frogs took away all the good

35

fishing, and how the Ghosts crept up to the village and stole away the sleep from his kinspeople's eyes. When he saw these things, he was very angry; and he called out to the Frogs and to the Ghosts alike:

"Old cowards, give back the fishing that you have stolen, and the sleep that you have taken away from the eyes of men!"

"Honq, honq," retorted the Frogs. "Whose talk is that? Honq, honq!"

"Tssee, tssee!" hissed the Ghosts. "Whose talk is that? Ha, tssee!"

"I am Tchamsem, and I have brought the box of daylight from the Oversky Country. Do as I say, old cowards, or I shall destroy every one of you; for, after all, ye are but lumps and shadows."

They stood still for a moment when he said that; but soon the biggest of the Ghosts cried out:

"Ha, great liar, do you think you can frighten us with such falsehoods? The box of daylight is kept by the Oversky Chief, and the man does not live who could so much as touch it with his little finger."

"I am the grandson of the Oversky Chief," replied Tchamsem, "and I have played with the sun-box ever since I could crawl."

Then they kept silence for a long time. But after a while their chief Frog cried out:

"Ha, honq! Great liar, if you really have the box of

daylight, open it, and we will believe you."

"That will I do," replied Tchamsem; "but only a very little, lest it burn up the whole world."

So he opened the box of daylight.

And as he did so, although the lid was raised only the breadth of a hair, there was a loud crackling sound, as of a lash when it curls out against the wind. The light shot forth in huge blinding waves, putting the Frogs to flight and destroying the Ghosts as spider-webs are destroyed by a hurricane. For, after all, they were but shadows.

Tchamsem quickly pressed the lid down with all his strength; but even then he could see the daylight leaking out in a thin steady stream, like smoke.

He pressed down the lid once more and sat upon it. Then he looked out over the river. Here and there he saw faint outlines, as of boats floating bottom side up. These were the capsized canoes of the Ghosts. As for the Frogs, they sought refuge with their cousins the Rocks; there they remain to this day.

After he had rested awhile, he went up to the village to see his kinspeople. They were frightened by the daylight and had all shut themselves up in their houses. Tchamsem went to the headman's house and knocked on the door.

"Who is that?" asked the headman.

"I am Tchamsem, and I have brought the box of daylight from the Oversky Country. I have scattered the

Frogs and destroyed the Ghosts. Henceforth ye shall have good fishing, and no fear shall disturb your sleep."

Then the headman of the village rose quickly and told all his people. So they gave a potlatch [1] for Tchamsem, and there was great rejoicing.

[1] Feast.

(X) : Tchamsem Gets the Halibut

In the early days of the world, there was no fresh water except what fell from the sky. The rivers were all brackish, and the people had to catch rain-water in great dishes, and sometimes there was not enough, and they perished with thirst. Nor was there any halibut, nor salmon such as we have now, and folks ate their food raw because they had no fire.

Then came Tchamsem from the Oversky Country, bringing with him the daylight in a round box; for before Tchamsem the whole earth was in darkness. After he had broken up the kingdom of the Ghosts, he gave the sun-box to the great bird Ginsâa, who flies across the sky with it every day and returns with it by night underground. Now Tchamsem saw the suffering of his people for lack of water and he heard that very far to the westward there was a big chief named Axemag, who owned all the fresh water in the world. And Tchamsem said to himself: "I will go to this chief and get plenty of water for my people."

Now, while Tchamsem was on his way to the place where the water was kept, he grew very hungry, and, looking down into the river, he saw a fish swimming near the shore. Its name was Masquail. Tchamsem hid behind some reeds and waited until the fish came in reach, and then put out his hand to catch it. But the fish darted away with all his might, for he was scared, and Tchamsem could get hold only of his tail. This he gripped as

hard as he could, for he was very angry. Now, before
that the fish had a small head and a large tail. But under
the fierce grasp of Tchamsem the tail became very thin,
and the head swelled up amazingly.

"Ha ha!" laughed Tchamsem. "Old big head! Thou
shalt no more be called Masquail, but Masquayil, the
Bullhead."

And this is why the bullhead is thick at one end and
thin at the other even to this day.

Tchamsem went on, and when it was about sunset, he
came to a part of the river which belonged to Chief
Cormorant. The chief was sitting in a canoe catching
halibut. Now, Tchamsem knew that Chief Cormorant
had a great deal of food, so he swam out to the canoe and
begged the chief to let him sit in the boat and watch the
fishing.

"Climb in," said the chief, never taking his eyes off
the water.

Tchamsem sat there a long time looking hungrily at
the fish in the bottom of the boat. Finally he said:

"Chief Cormorant, may I have one small fish to broil
for my supper? I am very hungry."

"Ni-gi!" grunted Cormorant. "You have come here
to take my fish, have you? Ni-gi! Wait until I fetch up
this fellow, and I'll pitch you overboard, you beggar!"

"Tset, tset," whispered Tchamsem to himself. "I
doubt that!" But he said nothing to Cormorant. After a

while he caught a bug and put it on Cormorant's neck.

"Mmm! ha!" said the chief. "Be kind enough to scratch that bug off my neck! I can't turn loose the line."

"With pleasure," said Tchamsem, taking the bug in his fingers. "Open your mouth and I will put it in."

"Ni-gi! No, no! Put it in the water."

"Well, I will do that if you say so, but don't you know you will never catch anything if you put a bug in the water? Besides, it's a good fat bug, and I think you would like it."

"Put it in my mouth, then," said Cormorant, opening his great bill. He was such a glutton that he would eat anything.

"Stick out your tongue," commanded Tchamsem; "I'll put it on your tongue."

"Ni-gi! No, no!"

"I will throw the bug in the water, then."

"Here!" cried the chief, and he thrust out his tongue.

"Ha ha! Great glutton!" cried Tchamsem, seizing the tongue with both his hands. "You would pitch me overboard, would you?" So saying, he gave the tongue a vicious jerk and tore it out by the roots.

Chief Cormorant screamed with pain and made a rush for Tchamsem, but the wily fellow dodged him three times, and after that the chief fainted. He tumbled over to one side, nearly upsetting the canoe.

Tchamsem threw water in his face, and after a while

"HA HA!" CRIED TCHAMSEM, SEIZING THE
TONGUE WITH BOTH HIS HANDS.

Cormorant opened his eyes. When he saw Tchamsem, he was very angry and tried to call him bad names. But he could only say: "Gogogo!" Then Tchamsem laughed.

"Should you like to have your tongue back, chief?"

Cormorant nodded and said: "Gogogo!"

"Well, you can have it," said Tchamsem, "on two conditions. One is that I am to have all the halibut I want for my supper. The other is that whenever my people want any, they can get it, provided that they leave a third of the catch for you. Do you agree to that?"

"Gogogo!" cried Cormorant, and he shook his head.

"Very well, then, I shall throw your tongue into the water."

"Gogogo!" screamed the chief, trying to get at him.

Tchamsem held the tongue over the side of the boat.

"Stand back or I'll drop it in," threatened Tchamsem. "Do you agree to my terms?"

"Gogogo," replied Cormorant, nodding his head.

So Tchamsem gave back the tongue, and Cormorant let him have all the halibut he wanted. But the tongue did not grow into place properly, so that the cormorant can only say "gogogo" to this day.

(XI): Tchamsem and Axemag

After suffering many hardships Tchamsem came to the country of Axemag, who owned all the fresh water in the world. Axemag lived in a huge stone house called Plenty Water and had a great many servants to wait on him.

Now, it happened that the water-chief was standing in the door of his house when Tchamsem came up.

"Welcome, stranger," said Axemag, with a smile. He had large teeth, white and highly polished. Tchamsem shuddered when he saw them.

"Can thy poor slave find a sleeping-mat here, and a bit of herring?" said Tchamsem in his humblest tones.

"Teno-keklenx!" answered the water-chief. "My poor dwelling is ever open to strangers, especially such as have traveled from a far country."

Tchamsem followed Axemag into his house, and they sat down to a bountiful supper. While they were eating, a slave brought in a beautifully painted bowl full of fresh water. The water was very clear and sparkling. Axemag took a sip from the bowl and then passed it to Tchamsem.

"Drink," said the chief.

Tchamsem took a deep draught; and so long had it been since he had tasted anything but water from stale cisterns and stagnant pools that the liquid went to his head and he began to wander in his talk. Soon he had drunk all the water in the bowl.

"More!" shouted the chief to his slave. And the slave went straightway into a deep cave under the house and came up with another bowlful.

By this time poor Tchamsem was quite stupefied with so much drinking. He took the bowl in his hands, but let it fall to the floor. It broke into a hundred pieces, and the water spilled out all over the chief's eating-mat.

Axemag was very angry at this and looked round for his big club, intending to brain him on the spot. But

Tchamsem, heedless of everything, collapsed against the wall, with such a foolish face that the chief stopped to laugh at him before taking his life. The chief laughed so heartily that he dropped the club on the floor, and then he changed his mind about killing Tchamsem.

"I will keep him here," said the chief. "He is a strong fellow. He will make a good slave."

Now Tchamsem had recovered his wits about this time, and heard what the water-chief said. But he did not open his eyes. He would pretend to be asleep, he thought, and then he might hear something useful.

"Let him lie where he is," said Axemag to his slaves. "Get my bed ready and I will go to sleep."

Tchamsem lay with one eye open, watching the water-chief. He noticed that the water-chief took off his bright-colored blanket before he went to sleep. And as he laid it aside, behold! the big chief became a little, shrunken dwarf. For it was a magic blanket. He looked very old and feeble, as if he had lived a hundred years beyond his time.

"I will wait until the water-chief is sound asleep, and then I will creep up and steal his blanket," said Tchamsem. "After that I can get plenty of fresh water for my people."

After a while Axemag began to snore very loudly. Then Tchamsem crept up to the magic blanket, his heart beating in his throat.

"Mmm-ah!" said the chief, and he stirred uneasily in his sleep.

Tchamsem stood still; and for a moment his heart did likewise. Then it pounded worse than ever.

Little by little Tchamsem crawled closer to the blanket. Just as he was almost in reach of it, the chief stirred again and reached for his big club, which was lying alongside of him. Tchamsem sprang back like a cat. But his beads rattled as he did so.

"Mmm-ah!" said Axemag, opening his eyes. "What was that?"

"Eh? eh?" cried Tchamsem, as if awaking from a sound sleep. "What was what?"

"That noise, slave."

"What kind of noise, uncle? Perhaps I turned over in my sleep."

"Be more quiet, boy," said Axemag, closing his eyes again.

Tchamsem lay very still after that and put his wits to work. He saw that the chief's club was of very stout wood, inlaid with abalone shells. It was a medicine club, and it never struck except to kill. He resolved that he would first get hold of the club, then the blanket.

"This time tomorrow," he said to himself, "I shall be master of Plenty Water."

(XII) : Tchamsem Gets Plenty Water

Before daylight Tchamsem slipped outdoors and found a stick of rotten wood, which he inlaid with mussel shells. This he brought back, hidden under his blanket.

At sunrise the chief got up and told Tchamsem to go and fetch some fuel. Then he went down into the cave under the house. As soon as his back was turned, Tchamsem took the medicine club and put the rotten one in its place. Then he carried the club into the woods, where he hid it under some leaves. After that he got a good supply of fuel and went back to the house.

"Teno-keklenx!" cried the chief, coming up out of the cave. "That is very good. I think I will keep you here. Ha! How do you like that?"

Tchamsem did not answer.

"I say, how do you like that?"

"I like it about as well as old thieves like honest work," replied Tchamsem.

"Ha! Great slave!" roared the chief. "What do you mean?"

And he seized the club and made a rush at Tchamsem, intending to kill him. He struck Tchamsem such a terrific blow that, had he wielded the medicine club instead of the one made of rotten wood, he would have dispatched his enemy at once. As it was, the club shivered into a hundred fragments and fell harmless. Then Tchamsem quickly seized the chief's blanket and tore it from his body before he could recover from his surprise. There he stood, a little hunch-back dwarf, very old and feeble.

"Aha," cried Tchamsem, stepping back and waving the blanket in great glee, "you would keep me as your slave, would you? And would kill me because I have a free tongue?"

"Give me my blanket!" piped Axemag, his voice shrill with rage.

"Never mind about that, old coward," returned Tchamsem, coolly. "We shall talk about that all in good time. But first let me go down into the cave where all the fresh water is kept."

Axemag led the way, still grumbling, and they went down, down, into the very bowels of the earth, where it was damp as a fog, and the rock walls wept silently, like old chiefs who tell their people about the lost glories of the clan. Down, down, down they went, until they came to a great cold place where there were numberless jars, all full of the most delicious fresh water. Farther yet, Tchamsem heard the gurgle, tinkle, of a spring and the prolonged crash of a waterfall.

"Is this all?" asked Tchamsem.

"Not quite," said Axemag. "There is a gallery underneath us."

"We will go down, then," said Tchamsem.

The next gallery was even larger than the first, and there were so many jars of water that one would grow tired of counting them.

"Is this all?" asked Tchamsem.

"Very nearly all," said Axemag. "There is one more gallery."

"We will go down," said Tchamsem.

Now, the third gallery was larger than the second. So vast was the number of jars of fresh water, all standing in endless rows, that if Tchamsem had begun to count

DOWN, DOWN, DOWN THEY WENT, UNTIL THEY
CAME TO A GREAT COLD PLACE WHERE THERE
WERE NUMBERLESS JARS.

those jars, I suppose he would have been counting yet.

"Is this all?" he asked.

"Yes," answered the chief.

"Good," said Tchamsem. "The jars of water in these three galleries, and half of all that shall flow into them hereafter, belong to me and my people. Do you agree to that?"

"No!" shrieked the water-chief, quite purple with anger.

"Very well, then; I shall go into the woods and get the medicine club, and you shall have a good dose of it."

And he told how he had made a sham club and had hidden the real one among the leaves.

Then Axemag began to tremble violently and begged for his life.

"That you may have," said Tchamsem, "but I must have the fresh water."

Axemag agreed; and Tchamsem gave him back his blanket. But the medicine club he kept, as a bond for the faithful carrying-out of their agreement.

So that is how Tchamsem obtained fresh water for his kinsmen upon earth.

(XIII): He Gambles for the Salmon

After Tchamsem had got the halibut and the fresh water, he heard that far to the westward, on an island at the mouth of the Nass River, was a tribe of Taboo men who owned all the salmon in the world, so he said to himself:

"I will go to that island and get plenty of salmon."

His friends loaned him their best canoe, and he set out. The tide was favorable at first, and he made good progress; but before long the tide changed. Then, row as he might, he could make no headway.

After a while a breeze sprang up from behind him, and he began to move forward a little. But he had been delayed so long that it was dark before he reached the island. Very steep and forbidding it looked, rising sheer out of the water without a tree in sight, and with the stars winking violently behind it. Tchamsem rowed a great distance along the shore, looking for a place to land. Everywhere the black brine steamed up against the cliffs and then staggered back all milky.

At last, when he was almost worn out, he found a place where there was a broad shelf of sand. Here he beached his canoe and started inland, having with him the magic club which he had taken from Axemag.

He had gone only a short distance when he saw ahead of him a great stone house, with lights inside and strange music. He went closer and looked in; and there he saw the Taboo people, the owners of the island. Some were eating salmon, some were dancing; but for the most part they were sitting on the ground, gambling; and it was horrible to see, they were so hideous.

Tchamsem watched them for a while; then he set his wits to work. He knew that the house was enchanted and that he could only enter it by strategy. So he ran thrice around the house, making a cry like a raven: "Qa! qa! qa!"

The music stopped. Tchamsem could hear the people whispering together. Then one of them said:

"It is the raven, bringing us good luck."

"To be sure," said another, "it is our friend the raven. Let him in."

So they opened the door, and Tchamsem entered, looking for all the world like a raven, in his blanket of black feathers.

"Welcome, Chief Raven," said the Taboo people; for the raven is always the friend of shamans and of them that work enchantments. "Have you brought us good luck tonight?"

"The best luck in the world," replied Tchamsem. And he drew forth the medicine club from under his blanket.

The Taboo people fell back when they saw it, for they knew at once that it was indeed big medicine.

"Aha," said one, "that is a good club you have there, chief."

"It might be worse," said Tchamsem, putting it back under his blanket, "but it looks very shabby now. A little blood would polish it up amazingly!"

When he said this, the faces of the Taboo people became very black and ugly.

"We are having a little game; won't you join us?" said their headman, with a hateful smile. The headman's name was Little-Chief-of-Canoe.

"To be sure," said Tchamsem. And he sat down by the

gambling-sticks.

Now the Taboo people were gambling for salmon; so Little-Chief-of-Canoe asked what he would put up for them to play for.

"This," said Tchamsem, fingering his medicine club, Little-Chief's eyes sparkled.

"And what will you put up?" asked Tchamsem.

"Salmon," answered Little-Chief-of-Canoe.

This was just what Tchamsem wanted him to say.

"How much?"

"Oh, three boatloads."

Tchamsem laughed.

"It would take all the salmon in the world to match this club of mine," he said.

"We will not play, then," said Little-Chief-of-Canoe, getting up.

Then one of his people, whose name was Grease-that-is-Sticking-to-the-Stones, came forward and said:

"I will stake my share of the salmon for your raven blanket."

And another, whose name was Dry-Boxes-in-which-Fish-are-Kept, said:

"I will stake my share of the salmon for those beads around your neck."

So they each came forward and staked their shares of the salmon for something of Tchamsem's.

Then old Dry-Boxes-in-which-Fish-are-Kept whispered to Little-Chief-of-Canoe:

"Gamble with him for his club; I will put medicine on the gambling-sticks."

Now, Tchamsem overheard this, but he heard it only for himself and said nothing.

Little-Chief-of-Canoe thought awhile. Then he said:

"I will stake my share"—it was nearly half—"I will stake my share of the salmon for that club which you carry."

"Agreed," said Tchamsem. "Shall I gamble with you first?"

"I will wait until the last," replied Little-Chief-of-Canoe.

So Tchamsem gambled with the Taboo people. Sometimes he won and sometimes he lost, but mostly he lost.

"Give me my beads," said one.

"Give me my raven feathers," said another.

"When I have played with the chief, then I will pay, and I will collect," said Tchamsem.

They all gathered close to the two players. Not a word was spoken. There was no noise but the clack, clack of the gambling-sticks, which meant life or death to Tchamsem, and wealth or poverty to the Taboo people.

At first the sticks favored Tchamsem. But afterwards, when the medicine began to work, they turned up for Little-Chief-of-Canoe. Tchamsem made his last play and lost.

"Give me the club," cried the chief, springing to his feet.

Tchamsem stood up also.

"Give him the club," yelled the Taboo people, crowding up closer.

"Take it!" cried Tchamsem.

So saying, he swung the medicine club in the air and brought it down with terrific force on the chief's head.

Little-Chief-of-Canoe sank like a log of wood.

"Get back, you thieves," hissed Tchamsem, as the others made a rush at him.

He struck the foremost, old Dry-Boxes, and the others paused, still muttering.

He touched the old man's body with his foot. Dry-Boxes groaned, for the club had barely grazed him and he was still alive.

"Open your hand," commanded Tchamsem.

Dry-Boxes obeyed, begging for mercy. The hand was full of gambling-sticks.

"Throw back your blanket," commanded Tchamsem.

Dry-Boxes obeyed. Hanging from his neck was a deer-skin bag. The bag contained big medicine.

"Ha! Great thief!" cried Tchamsem, giving him a contemptuous kick; "did you think you would work your frauds on Tchamsem, the Raven? Take this, it is what you get: fair blows for foul play. As for this fellow," he went on, turning to the body of the headman, "he has paid the penalty. His salmon are mine, and henceforth I am chief in his stead, though some of you may be minded to take punishment."

The Taboo people now dropped on their knees and implored mercy. Tchamsem agreed to spare them, on condition that they should send to his people once a year all the salmon that he and his kinsmen might need.

So that is how the big catch of salmon began coming once a year up to Nass River.

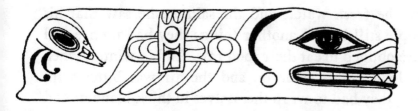

(XIV): The Town of the Air

After Tchamsem had obtained the daylight, the halibut, the fresh water, and the salmon, he saw that his people still lacked another thing: they had no fire and were obliged to eat their food raw. And in winter, when the long nights came on and the air was bitter with frost, they had to wrap themselves in thick blankets and creep into caves, like their friend the Bear: afraid to venture forth except for a little while at noon, upon very clear days.

Now, at that time all the fire in the world was owned by the Great Red Deer. The Red Deer lived in an enchanted forest very far to the north, and of the nine hundred men who had gone hither in search of him, only nine had returned alive. And none had brought any fire.

But Tchamsem, afraid of nothing upon earth, set out one fine morning for the house of the Red Deer, carrying with him nought but a few days' supply of rations and his trusty medicine club, which he had got from Axemag.

After long journeying he came to a very strange village, called the Town of the Air. By this time his provisions had given out and he was very hungry.

Tchamsem walked clear through the town without seeing a soul. A stray dog prowling between the houses was the only living thing that he saw.

Then he turned back, determined to find food if nothing else; for he was faint with hunger.

As he passed along the street, behold, the door of a house opened and shut of its own accord. He heard footsteps, but could see nobody. He stopped where he stood, and stared this way and that, a cold terror creeping over him.

Even as he looked, he saw a bundle of sticks floating as it were in mid air at about the height of a man's waist. The bundle made its way along the street until it came to the door of a certain house. There it stopped, and presently the door opened and the bundle of sticks went in. Then the door shut again.

Tchamsem could resist his curiosity no longer. Still trembling violently, he went to the door and, finding it unlatched, walked into the house.

Inside, it was somewhat dark, and at first he could see nothing. But soon he noticed, in one corner of the room, a red spark like a star. Tchamsem remembered that he had seen something of the kind many years before, in the Oversky Country; and then he knew that it was fire.

His heart beat fast, for he thought that he must be near his goal. He went closer to the fire, so as to get a better look at it; and as he did so, the bundle of sticks cast themselves upon it and burst into a hot flame. Then a pot of water got up and placed itself over the fire, just as if that were the most ordinary thing in the world. Vegetables that were lying on a shelf began to move about and, after rinsing themselves in another pot, hopped one by one into the boiling water. After a while a spoon got up of its own accord and began to stir the mixture.

Tchamsem was so amused by these queer antics that he forgot his fears, and when he saw the spoon rise gravely out of the pot and tap twice on the edge to free itself of the surplus liquid, he laughed aloud.

The spoon dropped heavily to the ground. There was dead silence for about the space of a heart-beat; then a voice said:

"Who is that?"

The voice was sweet and clear. A thrill, as of a new kind of terror, shivered Tchamsem from head to foot. At length he answered:

"I am Tchamsem, the Raven. I was born in the Over-sky Country and have come to earth to be the deliverer of my people. I am seeking the House of the Red Deer."

"And what dost thou here?" demanded the voice.

"I am faint with hunger. I have sought vainly through this town for a friendly face, and I find naught but empty terrors."

"Sit down, then," answered the voice. "When dinner is ready, you shall have something to eat."

Tchamsem did as he was told. Invisible hands lifted the steaming pot off the fire and ladled out the stew in deep dishes. One of these presented itself to Tchamsem. As he took hold of it, he felt for an instant the touch of warm fingers.

"And now," said the voice, when Tchamsem had appeased his hunger, "you had best be gone; and mind you say nothing to mortal or immortal of what you have seen or heard."

But Tchamsem lingered; for he was curious to know whence this voice proceeded.

"But who are you?" he asked.

"I am Evening Sky, and my father is chief of this village. You cannot see me because this is the Town of the Air, and I and all my people are invisible. But I can see you, and you have the manner of a great prince."

She spoke rapidly, stopping every now and then as if to listen for footsteps.

"Now go quickly," she added, giving him a gentle push that only rooted him to the spot; "—but stay, it is too late now! Here, get in this box."

Almost immediately he heard the chief and his men come in, asking for their dinner.

After a while the chief said:

"Daughter, why do you not give us clean dishes? This man says that his dish has grease sticking to the side."

"Well, father," replied the Princess, "it is good grease, is it not?"

At this the chief laughed and said no more about the dish.

After a while Tchamsem fell asleep. He slept a long time and dreamed that he was at his old home again, in the Oversky Country.

He was awakened by a touch on the shoulder. The lid of the box was raised, but he could see nobody. The house was very dark.

"You must go now," whispered the Princess. "My

father is asleep, and no one will see you on the street. If you want to find the House of the Red Deer, you must keep straight to the north for three days. Here is your club, but they will take it away from you before you can enter the forest."

She gave him her hand and helped him out of the box. His muscles were so cramped that he could hardly rise.

"This way," she said, leading him to the door. Outside, it was brilliant moonlight.

"Keep straight to the north—be very discreet," she cautioned, still keeping hold of his arm.

He felt her warm breath on his cheek. Their lips met. Then the door closed behind him and he was alone.

So he set out in the cold moonlight. But his heart was high in his breast; and so glad he was that he fell to singing:

> "Ho, ho, hi, hi!
> Ho, ho, ho, hi, hi, hi!
> Gyok, gyo, ghi, ghi!"

He went along in this fashion until he got to the edge of town. There he heard footsteps behind him, as of people running. He looked back, but could see nothing. He turned quickly to the left, hoping to elude his pursuers.

"Stop!" cried a voice directly in front of him.

A mocking laugh rang out, almost in his ear. He faced about and ran headlong, his knees melting under him. Soon an arrow sang past his shoulder, flicking a couple of feathers from his blanket. Then someone struck him a crashing blow in the chest. He staggered back, hitting

out wildly, but faced only blank emptiness. The same numb terror overcame him which had struck him nerveless the day before. He stood rigid, unable to move or speak, but, casting his eyes helplessly about, saw only the rude houses and the moon, wheeling solitary across the chill sky.

In a moment he was seized by both wrists in a grasp that was like copper chains, and a voice demanded:

"Who art thou? Why comest thou here to act the thief?"

"I am no thief," he answered, "and I have stolen nothing in your town. I am Tchamsem, the Raven, and I am on my way to the House of the Red Deer."

"And what wouldst thou do with the Red Deer?" asked another voice.

Tchamsem perceived that he had made a mistake in telling whither he was going; so he delayed answering this last question.

Then the first voice broke the silence:

"Let him go to the Red Deer, then; that will be the last of him, for he will not return alive. But let us see to it that he leaves our town, and in such manner that he will not be minded to come back."

At this there was a murmur of approval; and invisible hands began to buffet him about from all sides. His medicine club was taken from him, and he was quite powerless against his invisible enemies. Turn which way he might, he encountered savage blows, until he was bruised from head to foot. At last, half-fainting and covered with blood, he staggered over the town limit, where his persecutors left him. He sank down by the side of the trail and knew no more until the next day.

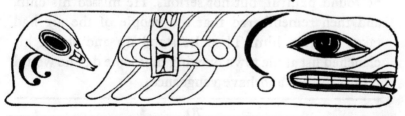

(XV) : Tchamsem Consults the Stump

When he awoke, Tchamsem felt as though all his muscles had been riveted together with copper pins. He got up with difficulty and took account of his hurts, which he found painful, but not serious. He missed his club, and then remembered that the people of the air had taken it from him. Then he stood up and shook his clenched fist at the town, vowing that some day he would return thither and have vengeance.

So he set out again, keeping straight to the northward, but he did not go far that day, nor the next, for every step gave him great pain. At nightfall of the third day he found himself in the outskirts of a great forest, and he lay down to rest under the shelter of a tree. About midnight the moon began to rise, and the air became filled with snow. Tchamsem awoke, shivering.

He reasoned that if he lay there much longer, he must perish with the cold. He got up, but did not know which way to turn. He had forgotten where the north was.

While he was still groping about amongst the trees, a red blush appeared in the sky ahead of him. Slowly it overspread the whole heavens. Long tongues of flame shot up from the horizon and then trickled back again, red, yellow, and deep blue. It was wonderful.

Then Tchamsem knew that he was on the right path; for those mysterious lights in the north were nothing more or less than the great fires kindled by the Red Deer.

As he looked he was very glad; his lameness vanished, and he became warm even to his finger-tips. Joyfully he pressed forward; and at length he felt the heat of the fire and even smelled the smoke. Then he went on until he came to a sort of clearing or open space, in the middle of which, a huge black square against the blinding flames, rose the House of the Red Deer. No man had ever entered it except by stealth, and no man had ever come out of it alive.

Now Tchamsem did not know how to proceed. So he sat down on a stump and buried his face in his hands, trying to think what he should do. After a while he heard a small voice that seemed to come out of the ground saying:

"Don't you think you have rested long enough? You are rather heavy."

Tchamsem stood looking down, very much perplexed. "And who are you?" he asked.

"Who should I be?" replied the Stump. "I have been here in this forest for a hundred years, and you have just arrived. It is you who should give an account of yourself."

"Well, I am Tchamsem, the Raven, if it comes to that. I was born in the Oversky Country, and I seek the great

Red Deer, that I may get fire for my people."

And he told all of his adventures, omitting nothing.

"You have a task ahead of you," said the Stump, when he had finished. "I have sat here for a hundred years, and the only person who ever obtained fire from Red Deer was Chief Echo, the Invisible."

Then the Stump, whose name was Amhats, told how the Red Deer slew all the people that came into his house, tossing them on his antlers; and how, in the fall of each year, he would get fire by striking his antlers on the trunks of the trees, thus kindling the great flames which people call the Northern Lights; which, as the winter wore itself away, would die down and finally go out entirely. And the trees would put forth new shoots and regain what they had lost by burning (for they were enchanted trees), so that, despite the vast fires every winter, the forest was never consumed.

"His power is in his antlers," said Amhats. "If you could touch his antlers with a medicine stone, you could always get fire from it."

"But how can I get the medicine stone?"

"The Red Deer has an ax, which he uses to split wood with. The head is of stone, and it is big medicine. What you must do is to steal this ax and strike the Red Deer's antlers with it."

"Alas!" cried Tchamsem, "that is more than I can accomplish. For to touch the antlers of the Red Deer is

"YOU HAVE A TASK AHEAD OF YOU," SAID THE
STUMP. "I HAVE SAT HERE FOR A HUNDRED
YEARS."

certain death. How much greater the peril, then, to strike them with his own ax!"

"The lightest blow would be sufficient," replied Amhats. "For my part, I would gladly see him struck dead, for he it was who reduced me to my present stature, and with that same ax. But to kill him is impossible. The man does not live who could slay the Red Deer, even though he wielded the club of Axemag."

Tchamsem smiled grimly, thinking for a minute of that formidable weapon, which the People of the Air had taken away from him. There he was, at the House of the Red Deer, and unarmed.

At first the thought discouraged him. Then it gave him new vigor. He would perform his latest and most perilous adventure without weapons of any kind. He would do by craft and by native strength what the sturdiest had heretofore failed in, even when aided by supernatural powers.

(XVI) : He Gets Fire from the Red Deer

So Tchamsem thanked his strange friend and crawled slowly to the door of the house, ready to spring backward at any moment and make his escape. The door was ajar; inside he saw the great Red Deer, fast asleep. Beside him lay his wife. The house was still, save for the crackle of a great fire heaped up in the middle.

Outside, it was bitter cold. Tchamsem pushed the door open a little wider and slipped in.

He looked about for the ax, but in vain. He thought it might be on the other side of the fire, the light of which blinded him. So he moved quietly to the left, and as he did so, his knee grazed against something, he could not see what. He put out his hand very carefully and found a black cord, stretched across the house like the trigger-string of a trap.

He looked up and faced the mild eyes of the doe, staring drowsily at him. Her master stirred uneasily in his sleep.

Tchamsem, still crouching, assumed an attitude of terror.

"The Bear!" he whispered hoarsely, pointing to the door. "Keep him out, for he is coming."

Now Tchamsem knew that the Red Deer feared but one creature upon earth; and that was the Northern Bear, whose home was in perpetual ice, and who at long intervals roamed southward, devouring everything in his path.

The doe started up at the word. For a moment she stood at gaze, her nostrils aquiver. Then, with one bound of her graceful body, she sprang to the door and closed it. And just at that moment, as if the elements themselves favored Tchamsem, a huge branch torn from one of the trees by the wind hurled itself violently against the house, so that the timbers groaned and trembled.

"The Bear!" shrieked the doe, now crazed with fright.

THE RED DEER AWOKE, AND SO VAST WAS HE
THAT HE SEEMED TO SURGE UPWARD LIKE A
GREAT CLOUD.

"The Northern Bear!"

The Red Deer awoke, and so vast was he that he seemed to surge upward like a great cloud. His antlers towered to the roof, branching against the rafters.

"Let me out," he said, "and I will give him battle!"

But the doe was before her lord in an instant, trembling piteously.

"No, no!" she cried, "stay here! Why should he harm us? Soon he will go away, and then we shall be none the worse."

The Red Deer tossed his antlers, but made no reply. Then he caught sight of Tchamsem.

"Who is this fellow?" he asked, pointing questioningly at Tchamsem.

"I don't know," answered his wife, "the Bear chased him hither—"

"And it was well that he did," put in Tchamsem, "for I should have been devoured by now, bones and all. Ah, he was hard upon me!"

And they could but believe him, so ashen was his face.

"Who are you?" repeated the Red Deer.

"I am Tchamsem, the Raven. I was beaten in yonder town by invisible ruffians, and scarcely had I escaped from them when I was chased by the Northern Bear."

"Welcome, then," said the doe, whose mild eyes had looked kindly on Tchamsem from the beginning. "And you will find shelter here for the rest of the night."

"Our poor dwelling affords but meager comforts," said the Red Deer, who was still suspicious of him. "However, such as they are, they are yours."

As he said this, a clever scheme occurred to Tchamsem.

The doe had now replenished the fire and gave their guest a few tender herbs, which he found good to the taste and very strengthening. While he ate, he talked, and so witty was he, and so good-humored, that the Deer and his wife—the latter especially—were highly entertained, and their suspicions of him vanished.

In this manner the rest of the night passed away pleasantly, until at daybreak Tchamsem noticed that the Red Deer was watching him again. The trap had been laid, but Tchamsem was careful not to walk over it.

By dint of great zeal in helping to pile on the wood Tchamsem had contrived that by this time their supply of fuel was exhausted. The Red Deer stirred uneasily when his wife announced that they needed more wood.

"We had best not unbar the door," observed Tchamsem, "until we are quite sure that the Bear is gone. He may still be lurking in the neighborhood. Now, if I could peep out through the smoke-hole, I could soon set your minds at rest. Can you give me a lift to the smoke-hole, chief?"

"I doubt if I could reach that high," answered the Red Deer.

"You might raise me on your antlers, then," suggested Tchamsem.

The Red Deer looked at him dubiously. But he wanted the firewood, and, above all, he wanted to be sure, before unbarring the door, that his enemy was gone. So he lifted Tchamsem on his antlers, until the man's head was through the smoke-hole.

"A little higher, chief," said Tchamsem. "I want to see the whole neighborhood. Thank you." And he crawled out on the roof.

In a moment he called back:

"The Bear seems to be gone, chief. I can see nothing of him— And since you have been so kind, why can I not cut some wood and save you the trouble? Pass up the ax, and I will have a few sticks directly."

There was no reply at first, and Tchamsem began to fear that he had ventured too far. He heard the Red Deer talking with his wife, who was still very much afraid. At last the handle of the ax appeared at the smoke-hole. The Red Deer was lifting it on his antlers.

Tchamsem seized the ax with both hands and, in lifting it through the smoke-hole, gave the antlers of the Red Deer a sharp blow as if by accident.

The sparks burst out in a little brilliant shower. The Red Deer withdrew his head with a loud cry of surprise and rage.

Tchamsem lost no time, but slid quickly off the roof

and dropped to the ground on the side farthest from the door, just as the Red Deer drew the bolt and stormed out in pursuit. Tchamsem knew that flight would be useless, as the man does not live who can outrun the Red Deer; so his only hope lay in strategy. He darted round the corner of the house and ran to the front, the Red Deer having meanwhile gone round the opposite way. Then Tchamsem, after looking this way and that, ran into the house again, where he found himself with the Red Deer's wife. The doe started, with a mild and half-frightened expression, backing meanwhile into one corner of the house.

"Quick! Bolt the door!" he panted. "He will kill me!"

The Red Deer's wife turned to look out at the door. This was what Tchamsem wanted. He slipped over to the other corner of the house and got behind the black cord that worked the trap. He was careful not to touch the cord, for he knew how easily the trap would open.

Scarcely had he done this when the Red Deer came in sight, shaking his antlers and fairly stamping the ground with fury.

"Here I am!" yelled Tchamsem. "What do you want?"

The Red Deer turned and came thundering into the house. So blind was his rage that he did not see the black cord, but ran violently against it. The earth yawned beneath him, and he crashed headlong into the deep pit which he had prepared for his enemies.

"Aha, old buck!" cried Tchamsem, calling down to him. "I suppose that I can now depart in peace. Well, good-morrow to you, and remember that you have a warm friend in Tchamsem, the Raven. May I have this ax as a memento?"

Without waiting for a reply he took his departure.

After many days he reached the Nass River and gave fire to his people, who received him with great rejoicing.

For a long time after that, Tchamsem's ax-head was the only place to get fire, and all the chiefs used to go to him for that purpose. But as the years went by, one chief after another said to him: "Prince, it is a great way that I have come; I beg of you, let me chip off a little piece from the edge and carry it to my own house." And Tchamsem allowed him to do this. So at length the whole ax-head was chipped away and scattered all over the country. People get fire from those little stones even to-day; and that is what they are; they are fragments of the medicine ax of Tchamsem.

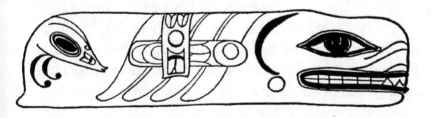

(XVII) : Little Pitch

After Tchamsem had taken the fire from the Red Deer, he stayed for many years with his people along Nass River. But at no time was he quite able to forget the invisible Princess who had saved his life in the mysterious Town of the Air. Nor did he fail to remember his magic club, which the invisible folk had taken away from him. At night, when the fire in his house died down on the slags, and its light flickered fitfully on the great costly skins hanging along the walls, Tchamsem fell to dream-

ing as he sat near the red embers, and each time that he
dreamed, he would say to himself: "Tomorrow I will
start for the Town of the Air." But when the morning
came and his companions began to whistle for him
betimes to follow them over the wild trails in search
of big game, he put off his journey until the next full
moon.

Thus, as I have said, many years slipped away. At last
Tchamsem, taking with him only a wallet of dried fish,
started northward to find the Town of the Air. As he
left his own village, he saw, very far overhead, the good
bird Ginsâa, flying across the sky with the sun-box in his
talons. Tchamsem put his hand to his mouth and called
with a loud voice: "Git! git! git! Ginsâa!" and the bird
as of old answered his cry: "Git! git! git! Good luck to
thee, Tchamsem, the Raven! But beware of Amala-
of-the-Smoke-Hole, the great dirty-faced chief who
sleeps with his head out of doors and has the pole of the
earth on his back, and of Little Pitch, who would steal
the world if he could hide it away."

Tchamsem thanked the bird and proceeded on his
journey. After a while he came to a house at the edge of
a very thick wood. He was tired and thirsty, so he
knocked on the door of the house; and as he did so, he
noticed that the door was very black, and that all the
posts of the house were black also. He knocked three
times before he could get an answer, but at last the door

opened and a perfectly black man, gorgeously dressed in eagle-feathers and abalone shells, asked him what he wanted.

Tchamsem told the black man that he was very tired and thirsty and would like a place to spend the night and have a small dish of salmon.

"Ho! ho!" said the black man, and his face glistened as he spoke. "You must think I am very rich, to be taking care of every idle fellow who chances to come along; but come in and tell me all about yourself."

Tchamsem went into the house; and there was the black man's wife, sitting by the fire and poking it with a long stick of wood. Tchamsem noticed that the black man would not go near the fire. Instead he sat down in a far corner of the house and began asking questions. Tchamsem answered them all as best he could without telling who he was or whither he was going, and meanwhile he noticed that his host perspired visibly on the side of his face that was nearest the fire. It glistened as if it were very wet. Tchamsem wondered for a long time who this might be, for he knew that he was some big chief, because of the fine skins and shells hanging along the walls; but not until his host took up a stick of wood and Tchamsem saw that his fingers left a black streak upon it did he know who the dark man was.

"Ho! ho!" said Tchamsem to himself, "this is Little Pitch, the big rich chief of whom I have heard so much.

Perhaps he will tell me something about the Town of the Air."

By this time supper was ready, and they all fell to with a will. The old woman, Little Pitch's wife, brought water for them to drink. Little Pitch would not come near the fire, but sat off in a corner by himself. When he lifted the drinking-bowl to his mouth, a curious scum ap-

peared upon the water wherever his lips touched it. The water shone in different colors, like a rainbow, when he had finished drinking out of the bowl.

"There is no doubt about it," said Tchamsem to himself; "this is Little Pitch, the great rich man." Tchamsem then told some of his adventures, and these amused the chief very much.

When he was in high humor, Tchamsem asked if he had ever been to the Town of the Air. The chief said: "Yes, many a time." Tchamsem drew a little closer when the chief said this, and it was plain that he was anxious to hear more. Now, all this while Little Pitch's own medicine club had been lying on the ground beside him.

Tchamsem was so interested that he did not notice that Little Pitch's eyes were fixed on him.

"Yes," said the chief, "I have been to the Town of the Air at least nine times. It is hard to get there, but yet harder to get away when once you arrive. Unless a person knows how to work medicine on these people, they will kill him without a doubt. I should never have got away the first time I went there had I not got advice from a shaman who loaned me big medicine and told me how to work it. You see, it is like this: You take a stick, this stick for example"—and he picked up the club—"and you dip it three times in the spring where a piece of the moon is. I will show you the spring, for it is not a day's journey from my house. Then, when you have done that, you paint it three times with red paint made from star-blood. If you have never seen any star-blood, I will show you some, for it is not above three leagues from my house. Then you let the stick lie out fourteen nights in the dew, with a squirrel-skin hanging from it. After that you are ready to start for the Town of the Air. You can hide the stick under your coat, and nothing on earth can hurt you. When you reach the Town of the Air, all you have to do is to hurl the stick at them, so!"—and he flung the club violently towards Tchamsem. The young man dodged just in time to save himself; but, as it was, seven hairs on his head were grazed, and they were white the rest of his life. Tchamsem recovered himself very quickly and darted after the club, but the old squaw, who was nearest to it, was there ahead of him. She grasped it in her long, bony hands and carried it back to her husband, making all the while very ugly faces.

Tchamsem now saw that he was in perhaps the greatest danger of his life. So long as Little Pitch had hold of the medicine club, he was entirely at his mercy.

(XVIII) : Little Pitch and Tchamsem

Tchamsem lay down and pretended to sleep, but all the time he kept one eye half-open and never lost sight of the black man. After a long time Little Pitch gave the medicine club to his wife and went out to catch halibut, for the night was very dark and still, and the river was full of fish. Little Pitch never fished in the day. The sun was bad for his health. In fact, it was said that if Little Pitch stayed long in the sun, he would melt and run into the ground. After Little Pitch was gone, Tchamsem lay very still for a while and then began to talk in his sleep. He noticed the old squaw was watching him and listening to what he said. Tchamsem talked about a great many things, mumbling to himself like a man in a trance. Finally he said:

"I see a very dark river. There are fish in the river. The moon is just rising behind the hills. I see a boat on the river. There is a man in the boat. He is a very large man, and his face is perfectly black. He seems to be catching halibut. I can see him very plainly. He is leaning over the side of the boat, drawing in great strings of fish. He is leaning *too far* over the side of the boat."

When he said this, the old woman bent forward, her eyes blazing with anxiety. She let go of the club, and it fell to the floor of the hut.

"I see a man," said Tchamsem again, "leaning out over the edge of a boat. He is leaning *too far* over the edge of the boat. There! He has fallen in. He is struggling in the water and is calling for help."

When he said this, the old squaw jumped up, leaving the club on the ground. Tchamsem was about to make a spring for it when she turned and picked it up. Tchamsem muttered in his sleep what sounded like curses, but the old woman did not hear. Tchamsem waited but a short time after she was gone; then he slipped quietly out of the house and ran towards the river by another way.

Tchamsem was much fleeter of foot than the old woman, so that he reached the river first. There he found Little Pitch in his canoe, stranded hard and fast on a sand-bank.

"Heh, neighbor!" cried Tchamsem, wading out to the canoe; "you seem to be having a dull time of it."

"Heh! heh!" grunted the old chief; "where did you come from?"

"Oh, nowhere in particular," said Tchamsem. "I dreamed you were in trouble, and thought I would come down and help you out."

"Well, if you will push my canoe off this sand-bank," replied the chief, "you will do me a great service."

"That will I do, and quickly," replied Tchamsem, for he saw over his shoulder the old squaw not more than three hundred paces off, staring at them and running forward at full speed through the bushes.

Tchamsem pushed with all his might at the canoe. Being a very strong man, he soon had it off the shore, and then he leaped into the boat with Little Pitch.

They caught a great many fish that night, and it was nearly daybreak before Little Pitch suggested that they start homeward. But Tchamsem knew that the old woman was running up and down the bank with the medicine club and he had no desire to meet her. Besides,

Tchamsem was determined to put Little Pitch out of his way, for he had tried to take Tchamsem's life and would do so again as soon as they reached shore. So the young man guided the canoe very deftly to a certain water where he guessed that they would run aground again. He knew that Little Pitch could not swim.

"Let us go home quickly," said the black chief, for he saw day beginning to break behind the hills.

"Oh, no," replied Tchamsem, "it is very early yet, and I do enjoy the early hours of morning."

"It makes no difference to me what you enjoy," said Little Pitch. "I, for one, am going home, and that quickly."

"Very well, then," said Tchamsem, "give me the paddle and I will get you home without delay."

Tchamsem then paddled along and ran fast aground on the shoal.

When Little Pitch saw that the canoe was aground, he was furious. He commanded Tchamsem to get out and push the boat off immediately. But Tchamsem declined to do so, saying that he wanted to enjoy the early hours of the morning. Little Pitch raged and fumed, but it was of no use. He tried to strike Tchamsem, but the young man was so much swifter of movement that he eluded him. Then the black man tried the force of argument, of flattery, and at length of piteous entreaty.

Meanwhile the sun had appeared in the sky and was

climbing higher and higher in the heavens. Still Tchamsem sat unmoved and talked eloquently of the glories of
sunrise.

Little Pitch began to perspire freely. His face shone
like the wet sea-cliffs when the waves tumble against
them. He sank feebly into one corner of the boat.

"Now," said Tchamsem, "you see what you get for
your perfidy. You tried to take my life and would do it
again if I put you ashore. What reason have I for putting
you ashore?"

"Every reason in the world," replied Little Pitch,
faintly. His nose was now melted off and his ears had
vanished entirely. "If you will put me ashore, I will
swear by all that is holy not to harm you. I will do more.
I will tell you how to get to the Town of the Air, and will
show you the spring where the piece of the moon is, so
you can make big medicine and overcome that town."

Tchamsem began to be sorry for Little Pitch, his
plight was so pitiful. The big chief was now so weak that

he could hardly move, and his voice had sunk to a whisper.

"I will tell you what I'll do," said Tchamsem; "I will swim ashore and tell your wife that if she will give me the medicine stick, I will pull the canoe off the shoal and put you in the shade, where you can get strong again."

"Do that, then, for the love of pity," said Little Pitch, "but lose no time about it, for I begin to feel my heart melting inside of my body."

Tchamsem then plunged into the river and swam ashore. He called to the old woman, who was some distance up the bank. When she saw him, she began to run towards him, brandishing the club.

"Stop," cried Tchamsem, "if you value your husband's life. He is melting to death in the canoe out yonder, and unless you at once give me that club, I refuse to push the canoe off the sand-bank and by noon he will be nothing but a black puddle in the bottom of the boat."

The old woman changed her tone at this and came up to Tchamsem whining piteously. She gave Tchamsem the club without more ado, and he promised faithfully to rescue her husband. He stuck the club in his belt and swam rapidly out to the canoe.

When he reached the boat, he found Little Pitch all huddled together and looking as if he had fainted dead away. His face was a sight to behold, being without nose, almost without lips or eyes. Tchamsem set to work at once and pushed the canoe off the shoal; then he quickly leaped aboard, and in a short time he had Little Pitch ashore under the shadow of the trees.

The old woman brought water from the spring and threw it over her husband, who began to show signs of life. At length he was strong enough to walk back to the house, where he lay down in the darkest corner and went fast to sleep.

It was nightfall before Little Pitch awoke. He was badly disfigured, but otherwise as strong as ever. When Tchamsem had reminded him of his promise, he took the young man about a quarter of a mile into the woods and showed him the spring with a piece of the moon in it. Tchamsem cut a rod of alder and dipped it three times into the spring. And Tchamsem gave back the medicine club to Little Pitch.

Afterwards he and Little Pitch went to the place where the paint was, and they painted the stick three times with star-paint.

This star-paint may be found in the country of the Eagle clan to this day. It is supposed to be the remains of a red star that fell to earth many ages ago.

(XIX) : The Dancing-Blanket

Early next morning Tchamsem walked on alone, hoping to reach the Town of the Air before nightfall; but this he was not destined to do.

As he was going through the woods, he saw hanging ahead of him what seemed to be a beautiful dancing-blanket. It was red and yellow and very magnificent. Tchamsem was glad when he saw this; and he sang:

"The supernatural gods are good,
I found a blanket in the wood—

A dancing-blanket bright and gay.
I'll throw my old dark shawl away.

"My old dark shawl, so dull and worn,
Me well through many a year hath borne;
But I shall wear it not henceforth,
I've found one now of greater worth.

"My raven blanket, coarse and black,
Hath no place on a rich man's back;
I've found a blanket bright and gay—
I'll throw my old dark shawl away!"

So he ran ahead to take the new blanket. As he ran, he tore off the old raven blanket and flung it far from him. And the color of the new dancing-blanket was as of clean copper, and star-paint, and fire. Never had he beheld a garment so beautiful.

But when he got close to the dancing-blanket, behold! it was no blanket at all; nothing but autumn leaves. Withered autumn leaves they were, and a spot of sunshine had fallen on them so that they looked like a splendid blanket.

Tchamsem was so disappointed and ashamed that he wept bitterly, for now he had nothing to put on. His raven blanket he had torn in shreds as he threw it away.

Painfully he gathered up the odds and ends and tried

to piece them together. But he could not do so. The night came on, and still he stood there, weeping and shivering, trying to put together the raven blanket that he had thrown away. None would have recognized him as Tchamsem, the great chief, hero of many exploits.

At daybreak came the good bird Ginsâa, who in very ancient times had perched twice or thrice on the shoulders of the high supernatural gods. He had never ceased to carry the box of daylight across the world after Tchamsem had intrusted it to him.

He was amazed at Tchamsem's plight and called down to the chief:

"Git-git-git Ginsâa!"

And Tchamsem answered, as of old: "Git-git-git Ginsâa!"

"Why so discouraged?" asked the bird. "And what has happened to your raven blanket?"

Tchamsem told him the story—all in a loud voice, for the bird could not come down, but must needs make his daily journey with the box of daylight.

And the good bird Ginsâa made answer and advised Tchamsem to go back to his own country and sit down patiently and sew his raven blanket together, just as if he had never been a rich chief at all.

Tchamsem took the good bird's advice; for had not Ginsâa at one time perched on the shoulders of the high supernatural gods? And he returned to his own country and to his own house; and he sat down patiently to sew together his raven blanket that he had torn in shreds. And thereafter he was wiser and more thoughtful.

(XX) : Tchamsem and the Tides

In those early days Tchanegoa, the Tide Woman, who lived in a great stone house at the edge of Ocean, owned the tides and held them back with her tide-line. So they turned only once a month instead of twice daily, and the people could not gather clams and sea-eggs because the tides were held by the Tide Woman.

The people begged Tchamsem to fare forth and make the Tide Woman let go the tide-line once a day, so that the clams and sea-eggs would be left on the beach for food.

"You have got us the daylight and the fresh water, the halibut, the salmon, and the fire," they said; "but the great tides of Ocean, that should bring us sea-food daily, are in the hands of Tchanegoa, that old witch, whose heart is as hard as the rocks whereon she perches. Brave indeed you are if you can overcome Tchanegoa, the Tide Woman."

Whereupon Tchamsem answered not a word, but early next morning he put on his raven blanket and flew forth in the high glittering sunlight until he came to the cliffs of Ocean, where dwelt the Tide Woman in her ancient stone house.

Now the Tide Woman's house was on a promontory that looked out over the sea, and Tchamsem alighted on a jagged ledge of rock just underneath. At the edge sat the Tide Woman, that aged giantess; and she had held the tide-line since the high supernatural gods last visited these earthly regions. (Every half-eternity or so the high supernatural gods come down and rule the world in person; then it is that all wrongs are righted, and there is peace and plenty over all the earth.)

Her legs were drawn up like a mountain; her face was weather-beaten and scored with storms; her hair floated to the wind like hoary dry seaweed. Such was Tchanegoa, the Tide Woman.

THE TIDE WOMAN'S HOUSE WAS ON A PROMON-
TORY THAT LOOKED OVER THE SEA. TCHAMSEM
ALIGHTED JUST UNDERNEATH.

Tchamsem called out in a loud voice:

"Hai! hai! Old witch, old woman, old giantess! You have held the tides long enough, and my people are in sore need. For they cannot gather the clams, the sea-eggs, the good food that they desire; only once a month may they gather it, and rightfully they should gather it once a day. Come now, let go the tide-line, that I may feed my people! Hai! I am Tchamsem, the Raven. I brought the daylight from the Oversky Country. I have obtained the fresh water, the halibut, the salmon, and the fire; now I shall get the tides."

But the roar and reduplicating crash of the waves drowned the voice of Tchamsem. The Tide Woman sat unheeding, and she stared motionless at the long, staggering brine.

High in the heavens wheeled Gull. He laughed a screaming laugh at the futile speech of Raven.

Then Tchamsem, the Raven, the crafty, the undefeated, had recourse to strategy.

He climbed down the steep rocks and went to the spruce forest that overlooked the sea on the other side. There he gathered spruce needles, a whole armful. Then he made his way back to the house of Tchanegoa, the Tide Woman.

Very cautiously he approached the house from behind. The wind and spray beat hard in his eyes, so that he could scarcely see. The laughter of Gull came down in short stabs. A cloud suddenly shut out the sunlight.

Step by step Raven approached the Tide Woman, seated before her house. Gull screamed at her from the sky:

"Tchanegoa! Tchanegoa! Beware of Tchamsem!"

But she was absorbed in her old oceanic dreams and did not hear.

At length Tchamsem perched lightly on the Tide Woman's spine, just where her salt-rimed cloak was gathered upon it. Lightly he dropped against her back the armful of spruce needles.

So the Tide Woman, for the first time in a thousand years, reached forth to scratch her spine. And she let go the tide-line, and the tide rushed out rebellowing and left much sea-food on the beach. She stretched her legs and turned and twisted in her efforts to get rid of the spruce needles. Now it was Tchamsem's turn to laugh.

"Aha, grandmother!" he cried, waving his dark blanket before her eyes. "A giantess you are, and with a gigantic itch! What would you give, grandmother, to get rid of the spruce needles?"

Tchanegoa did not reply, but she paused in her writhing and looked at Tchamsem.

"Loosen the tide-line every day," said he, "and I will take the spruce needles from your back so that you can rest in peace."

Solemnly the Tide Woman nodded. And Tchamsem took away the spruce needles. Not a sound uttered Gull from the heavens, for his rival had achieved another ex-ploit.

(XXI) : Tchamsem Gambles with Gull

You will remember how, when Tchamsem was disputing with Tchanegoa about the tides, his friend Gull was flying overhead, screaming with laughter. Now, Gull knew where all the herring came from—those wonderful fish from which people get such quantities of oil. But the Olachen Chiefs were very stingy in those days, and they kept the herring for themselves, and only a few were available for Tchamsem and his people. He had long desired to visit the country of the Olachen Chiefs, but Gull alone possessed the secret, and he would tell nobody. Now and then Gull went to this obscure place and filled himself with herring. When he returned, he would be so replete that he would disgorge one fish as he flew, and it would fall on the beach. This was the only way in those days that people obtained any herring at all.

Tchamsem resolved that he would visit this strange country and get plenty of herring for his people. But first he had to induce Gull to share the secret of the way to go there.

Now, he knew that Gull's one weakness was gambling. Tchamsem was a great gambler himself, but not for the joy of the thing; only when he was sure of winning would Tchamsem gamble—though he did risk much when he gambled for the salmon with the supernatural beings, as we have seen.

So Tchamsem made an elaborate set of gambling-sticks. Wonderful sticks they were, beautifully carved and painted. And he waited until he knew that Gull would fly past, and he began to play with the sticks, all by himself.

"Hai! Hai!" screamed Gull. "What are you doing?"

"Gambling with myself," calmly replied Tchamsem. And he continued to play with the sticks.

"Is that all you can do?" taunted Gull, swooping near. "And are you afraid to play with anyone else, for fear you might lose?"

Tchamsem did not answer at first, but kept on playing.

"I think I should rather play alone," he said at length.

"Ha ha! Great coward!" cried Gull. "Poor player that you are, small wonder that you wish to gamble with yourself. Ha! Great coward!"

"I am not a coward," returned Tchamsem, in an injured tone. "And I am not so poor a player as you think."

"Prove it, then!" screamed Gull. "Dare you gamble with me?"

"We had best get other sticks," said Tchamsem, hastily. "These might get spoiled. Let me run home and fetch my other set."

"Aha!" cried Gull. "Not so fast. We will gamble with the sticks you have in your hand. If they are fair for you when you gamble with yourself, they are fair enough for both of us when you gamble with me." (Now, this is just what Tchamsem wished him to say.)

"All right, then," Tchamsem agreed, with pretended reluctance. "But what shall we gamble for?—I have it! I shall risk my medicine club, and you shall risk—nothing! Only if you lose, you shall show me the way to the herring country, so that I may get herring for my people."

After a moment's hesitation Gull agreed; for he believed that Tchamsem was no match for him, and he wanted the magic club.

But the gambling-sticks of Tchamsem were of his own making.

So they gambled. And Gull lost; and he showed Tchamsem the way to the country of the herrings.

(XXII) : Bright-Cloud-Woman

Very strange were the instructions that Gull gave to Tchamsem, how he might reach the country of the Olachen Chiefs and get herring for his people.

"First you must make a small canoe of elderberry wood," said Gull. "Then smear the inside of the canoe with spawn of herring. I will give you one herring, which you can use. When you have done this, get in the canoe and let it carry you whithersoever it will. After so long a time you will come to the country of the Olachen

Chiefs. Now, these chiefs are four in number. The first is named Half-Eaten-by-Goose; the second is named Bursting Cloud; the third, Hot Stones; and the fourth, Boiling Box. But of all four Chief Bursting Cloud is the most crafty, the most terrible; see to it that you provoke him not."

Tchamsem thanked his friend Gull and proceeded to do as he was told. And the canoe sped swiftly down the river to the salt sea, and after many days Tchamsem came to the country of the Olachen Chiefs.

The first to come and look at the canoe was a very clever Mouse, whom the Olachen Chiefs were wont to send forth when they wanted to find out anything. Mouse, after smelling and nibbling about, reported that the canoe had been full of herring. Whereat old Half-Eaten-by-Goose, the ugliest (and stupidest) of the chiefs, cried:

"How can he have herring, when we own all that there is?"

Chief Hot Stones fetched an angry snort and said: "Some thief has stolen them from us."

But Boiling Box began to rumble something about mice being poor judges of fish, anyway.

Then old Bursting Cloud, that most depraved as well as most sagacious of the four chiefs, unsmiling shook his head and augured:

"Be not fools. It is Raven. He has already stolen the

daylight, the fresh water, the salmon, the halibut, and the fire, besides outwitting the Tide Woman; now he is after our herring."

"Ahai! ahai!" yelled Half-Eaten-by-Goose. "He is after our herring; let us bite his head off!"

"Yaho! yaho!" howled Hot Stones. "He is after our herring; let us roast his ears and his tongue, all chopped up very fine together!"

"Ngow! ngow!" rumbled Boiling Box. "It is Raven, and he is come for our herring. Let us pluck his eyes out and cook them well and eat them with stewed cranberries!"

Old Bursting Cloud was silent for a long time, even after the others had got through with their raving.

"He *has* herring already," said the chief. "I must ask

my friend Gull about this—how it is that others besides ourselves have any herring."

Now Tchamsem had followed Mouse to the village of the Olachen Chiefs, and he heard all this from where he was hidden behind the herring-house. For the Olachen Chiefs kept all the herring in a great house, just out of reach of the tides. So he put his wits to work, how he might set at naught the hostile plans of the chiefs and at the same time carry out his project of getting the herring for his people.

Old Chief Bursting Cloud had a daughter, and her name was Bright-Cloud-Woman. She was very bright and fair. Even while Tchamsem pondered, she went softly down to the beach, where his canoe was; for the little Mouse had told her also, and she was consumed with curiosity, as is the manner of females. When she reached the canoe, she went and perched in the stern of it. And Tchamsem saw this from where he was hiding.

So Tchamsem made haste, and ran to the beach as soon as the four chiefs had gone their way. Bright-Cloud-Woman saw him coming, and she was filled with amazement. For she had never beheld a young and good-looking man, only the chief her father, who was old and wrinkled, and the other chiefs and their servants, who were ugly beyond description.

Tchamsem saw instantly that this was his chance; and

TCHAMSEM TOOK BRIGHT-CLOUD-WOMAN IN HIS
ARMS AND KISSED HER.

he resolved to make the most of it.

"Little sister," he said softly, "be not afraid; I am Tchamsem, and I am come to marry you."

Then Bright-Cloud-Woman looked at Tchamsem, so tall and handsome in his raven blanket, and straightway she loved him. And she said:

"Welcome, Tchamsem. Gladly would I be your wife; but the chief my father has vowed that I should marry no one unless he be richer than Little Pitch, the great rich man."

"Ah, that is easily managed, my dear," replied Tchamsem; "for I am he to whom Little Pitch gave more than half of his goods."

"Ah, well, then," said Bright-Cloud-Woman, much relieved, "we will go to the chief my father and ask for his blessing."

So Tchamsem took Bright-Cloud-Woman in his arms and kissed her. And together they went and sought the old chief.

When he saw them coming, Bursting Cloud was very angry, and he well merited his name, for it seemed as if he would indeed burst apart under his blanket, he was so furious.

"Ha! Raven!" he thundered. "How dare you? How dare you walk with my daughter? Great liar! Thief! Beggar!"

"Liar and thief I may be," retorted Tchamsem, "but

beggar I am not. It was I who stole the box of daylight from the Oversky Chief, and I admit cleverly outwitting the Taboo people and the master of Plenty Water. But again it was I with whom Little Pitch, that great rich man, divided all his goods."

When Bursting Cloud heard this, he invited Tchamsem to come into his house; and he spread blankets, and they sat down.

"Tell me truly," said the chief, "are you as rich as all that? For I must say that I suspected you of coming here to steal our herring."

Tchamsem laughed. "What would I want with your herring, when I already have more than I and my people can use—besides the halibut and the salmon, of which we have plenty. If you don't believe it, look at my canoe; it has carried so much herring back and forth that it smells like herring in spite of everything."

But the old chief was still unconvinced, and he asked for time to think it over. What he really wanted was to wait until Gull came again, so that he could get the facts.

After many days Gull arrived on one of his regular visits to the country of the Olachen Chiefs. And old Bursting Cloud asked him privately about Tchamsem's canoe, and whether he really owned any herring.

Now, in his heart Gull hated the old man, whom he thought very stingy. And he bore no grudge against Tchamsem. So he said:

"Herring? Herring? He owns so much herring that his people dry all but the best and use them for fuel. His canoe had just fetched a boatload when he started. I saw it myself."

At this the chief was completely satisfied and his suspicions were swept away. And he consented to the marriage of Tchamsem and Bright-Cloud-Woman and gave a great potlatch, the like of which was never seen; nor has it ever been surpassed, even to this day.

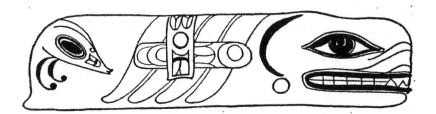

(XXIII) : Tchamsem Obtains the Herring

Tchamsem lived with Bright-Cloud-Woman for nearly three months, and she loved him dearly. One morning he said : "Wife, I fear that you do not care for me as much as you did when we were first married."

And she, anxious to please him, replied: "I do, my dear; I do indeed. I care for you not less, but more than ever."

But Tchamsem was not so easily pacified. "Prove it,

then," he grumbled. "If you really love me, you will do whatsoever I ask."

"Oh, gladly, my dear," responded Bright-Cloud-Woman; for she fancied he might ask for a thousand kisses or some similar gift, equally delightful in the giving as in the receiving.

"Well, then," said Tchamsem, "I want the wooden bar that holds the door to the herring-house."

"Oh, but you can't have that," said his wife, quickly.

"What did I tell you?" flared Tchamsem.

Bright-Cloud-Woman threw her arms around his neck.

"Be not angry with me, my love!" she cried. "But what you ask is not mine to give! The chief my father sleeps with one toe out of his blanket, and this toe is hitched up with the door of the herring-house by a slender thread, very strong, made of the sinews of a tomtit."

"So much the better," said Tchamsem, calmly. "You, and only you, can sever this thread and get me that which I desire."

"Ah, dearest husband, you know not whereof you speak. Did you ever try to cut in twain the sinews of a tomtit? So tough they are that no knife can ever sever them save after much hacking and straining. Whereat my father would awake, and we should all be done for."

Tchamsem rose. "You, with your woman's ingenuity, can solve the matter if you will," he said; and he walked angrily away.

His wife was truly grieved, and quite at a loss, for she loved her good-looking husband and was distressed at not being able to please him.

Now, Bursting Cloud coiled up his thread every morning when he awoke and put it away to use the next night. So Bright-Cloud-Woman took our friend Mouse into her confidence. And, with promise of rich reward, she made Mouse nibble and gnaw the sinews of the tomtit every night at a certain point just outside the chief's house; and Mouse nibbled and gnawed so gently that old Bursting Cloud did not awake. And each night the tomtit's sinews were that much nearer to being gnawed asunder.

At last the Mouse came to her one night and whispered that the thread was severed. So Bright-Cloud-Woman rose quickly and went and brought one end of the sinews of the tomtit, of which the other end was fastened to the bar on the herring-house door, and gave it to her husband, saying:

"Here, my love; do but follow this thread and you shall have what you wish."

Whereupon Tchamsem kissed his wife and embraced her tenderly. But, instead of following the thread to the herring-house, he grasped the end firmly and went to the beach, bidding his wife to follow. There they got together twoscore canoes and ranged them along the beach, all tied one to the other with the sinews of the tomtit, ready to be launched.

Then, while Bright-Cloud-Woman yet wondered, Tchamsem gave the thread a most terrific jerk, so that only the sinews of a tomtit could have stood the strain. And at the other end the bar was pulled out from the door of the herring-house, and the whole house burst open, and it seemed as if all the herring in the world were pouring downhill to the beach for Tchamsem and Bright-Cloud-Woman to load into the canoes.

(XXIV) : Oil Woman

A busy time of it had Tchamsem and Bright-Cloud-
Woman, loading the herring into the twoscore canoes.
But in a surprisingly short while they had the canoes all
full, and Tchamsem and his wife each got a huge paddle
and made ready to start. First he pushed off the canoes
into the sea, one after another, while his wife sat in the
stern of the forward one (the little elderberry boat) and
held it firmly to the shore lest the string of them drift
away. Then Tchamsem got into the canoe in front of her

and pushed off; and behold! out to sea went the long line of canoes loaded with herring, with Tchamsem and his wife in the first one, paddling hard.

So they paddled with long, vigorous strokes, both Tchamsem and Bright-Cloud-Woman—for she was nearly as strong as her husband—and with the forty boatloads of herring trailing behind them, until the dawn began to streak red in the east, and still there was no land in sight. And they began to be very weary with that hard paddling.

At length Bright-Cloud-Woman sank back in the boat and would paddle no longer. After some hours Tchamsem likewise gave up exhausted. But when he ceased paddling, lo! the prow of the canoe ceased not to cut the water into fine spray, and they went forward as before.

Then Tchamsem remembered that the elderberry canoe had brought him hither of its own will, and that it was big medicine. And he told his wife, and they both rejoiced greatly.

Soon after that, they came ashore; and the land was called Little Crabapple Place. This was the home of Oil Woman, and she came out to meet them, her face very dark and exceedingly shiny with oil.

Now, when Oil Woman saw Tchamsem, how young and handsome he was and how strong, she loved him greatly and resolved to take him away from Bright-Cloud. For Oil Woman was a sorceress, well versed in

BEHOLD! OUT TO SEA WENT THE LONG LINE OF
CANOES LOADED WITH HERRING, WITH TCHAM-
SEM AND HIS WIFE IN THE FIRST ONE, PADDLING
HARD.

supernatural arts and in the practice of many subtle poisons. And she chose the subtlest and the most deadly poison of all, which is the juice of the slander-berry, wherewith to dissolve the wedlock of Tchamsem and his wife, so that Oil Woman could have him for her own.

But Oil Woman pretended to be fond of Bright-Cloud and she received them both very kindly and gave them a house to live in and took care of their herring.

One day our friend Gull dropped down for a visit, on his way to and fro between the mainland and the country of the Olachen Chiefs.

"Aha, my dear!" cried Gull, that great good fellow, coming up to Bright-Cloud-Woman. "So I have found you at last. The chief, your father, will be very glad."

And Gull took her hand, in that friendly way of his, and kissed her. Whereat Oil Woman whispered to Tchamsem: "Did you see that, how Gull kissed your wife? They have been coming to this place together for many years."

Tchamsem was much enraged when he heard this, but he said nothing.

Soon afterwards he noticed that Oil Woman had some cooked herrings for supper, whereas he and his wife did not know how to cook theirs and had been eating them raw.

"I pray you, tell me how to cook my herring," he said to Oil Woman.

"Small profit to me whether I eat my herring cooked or raw, for I am quite alone in the world," answered Oil Woman; and she began to weep.

Like all strong men, Tchamsem could not resist the tears of a female. So he kissed her gently and stroked her hair, but she would not be comforted.

Oil Woman had contrived for Bright-Cloud to see this performance from afar. Whereat Bright-Cloud was wild with jealousy, and that night she said to her husband:

"Tell me, why do you kiss and embrace Oil Woman? Am I not your wife? Why are you faithless?"

Tchamsem, taken unawares, lied clumsily, after the manner of husbands; the truth would have served him better, for he cared naught for Oil Woman, except to learn how to cook his herring.

Whereat Bright-Cloud-Woman impaled him mercilessly on his own falsehood.

Then Tchamsem became very angry. "And who are you, to be casting stones at your husband? Have you not deceived me from the very start? Is not Gull your lover? And did I not see him kiss you less than a week ago?"

At this Bright-Cloud-Woman wept and screamed, and declared that she would go back at once to the chief her father. The poison of the slander-berry had done its work.

When Gull went back to the country of the Olachen

Chiefs, he carried a message to old Bursting Cloud from his daughter, telling him where she was and begging him to come and take her away from that rascally husband of hers, Tchamsem.

So in a short while came the old chief, with a number of his men, and he demanded of Tchamsem the return of his daughter, Bright-Cloud-Woman. But Tchamsem, who was really not anxious to get rid of his wife, saw a chance for bargaining.

"Ha, chief," he replied, "would you rob me of my dear wife, whom I love, and with no compensation at all?"

Wherefore they began to trade, and when they had traded awhile, they began to gamble; with the result that the old chief took back his daughter, and in return Tchamsem was to receive half of all the herring every year for his people.

(XXV) : Tchamsem Learns
How to Cook Herring

After Bright-Cloud had gone back home with her father, Tchamsem remained with Oil Woman, but was churlish and indifferent. So Oil Woman said to him:

"What is the matter, my dear? You go about with such a long face, and you never kiss me any more."

"Ah," sighed Tchamsem, "alas, my people have no herring, and it grieves me to think how perhaps they are starving."

"That can be easily remedied, my love. We will hitch the forty boatloads to the elderberry canoe, and it will bear them back to your people."

"We might try something of the sort," returned Tchamsem. "But in the mean time I am eating my herrings raw, for I know not how to cook them at all."

Whereupon Oil Woman, who was madly in love with Tchamsem and could deny him nothing, told him how to cook the herring:

"You must heat stones; and when they are red-hot, pour four pails of water into a large cedar box." Thus spake Oil Woman to Tchamsem. And she said: "Make a pair of tongs of cedar-wood for handling the red-hot stones. The tongs should be a fathom and a half long. Throw red-hot stones into the box; and when the water boils, fill five baskets with herring: then heat some more stones; and when they also are red-hot, make a large spoon of alder-wood, and use it for taking the stones out of the cedar box. When you have done this three times, the fish will be cooked. Pour more water in the box before you take out each lot of stones. And when you have put in the third lot, the oil will appear on top of the water; you will have all the grease you want."

So Tchamsem thanked Oil Woman when she had left off speaking, and he kissed her tenderly. She was very dark, of an olive complexion, and her hair was quite black. Tchamsem was thought by some to be dark, by reason of his raven blanket; but in truth he was light-haired, a very fair blond. This was because he was born in the Oversky Country. The Oil Woman thought that Tchamsem's hair was beautiful, but rather too curly. So she undertook to comb it out. She made a fine comb, es-

pecially for the purpose, and she combed Tchamsem's hair with it. But all the while he was planning how he might get back to his people.

They dried all the herring, Tchamsem and Oil Woman, and they packed it in the twoscore canoes. And he promised that he would take her with him, for she could not bear him out of her sight for an instant.

Six mornings, very early, Tchamsem rose up before Oil Woman was awake, and went down to the beach to make his escape. And six times his heart failed him and he crept back to Oil Woman's house.

But on the seventh morning he climbed resolutely into

the elderberry canoe and made fast to the stern the sinews of a tomtit, wherewith the forty boatloads of herring were strung out, and said to the elderberry canoe:

"Gunax haa! Gunax haa!"

And the canoe moved swiftly through the water, for those were supernatural words, and, as we have said before, the canoe was big medicine.

So Tchamsem returned to his own people with the forty boatloads of herring. And they rejoiced greatly. But whereas he reckoned that he had been away less than six months, behold, he found that he had been with Oil Woman three years; for she was a sorceress.

(XXVI) : The Four Chiefs of the Winds

There are four great chiefs in the four corners of the world. First there is North Wind, who wants the world to be always cold and pale. The Master of the South Wind wants it to be green, and so does the East Wind. The West Wind is gentlest of them all, and in ancient times he agreed with his two brothers East Wind and the Master of the South Wind; but with the eldest brother,

North Wind, none of them agreed: and North Wind hated his brothers bitterly.

So the East and West Winds and the Master of the South Wind made war on their brother the North Wind. Therefore the weather was very disorderly, and none could predict for one day ahead, winter or summer, whether it would blow hot or cold, wet or dry. People could neither plant nor plan; the world was topsyturvy and in a state of perpetual storm and turmoil.

Now, the Master of the South Wind had five children. The eldest was called Proud Rain; the second, Scowling Face; the third, Rain-Under-the-Knee; and the fourth son was named Going-Behind-Mountains. The youngest was a girl, and her name was Drops-of-Fresh-Water. The Master of the South Wind was the greatest of the four chiefs. Hence it came about that the Master of the South Wind, with his four turbulent sons, at length gained the ascendancy, and the weather was wretched and rainy almost without interruption.

The elder of the two sons of West Wind was named Evening Smoke; and the younger, Yellow Cloud.

East Wind likewise had two sons—Cloud-on-the-Mountain and Pink-Morning-Vapor.

North Wind had twin boys, Icehead and Frozen. Icehead and Frozen were both in love with Drops-of-Fresh-Water, but her brothers did not want her to marry a son of the North Wind.

At length came Tchamsem the Raven to the house
of the South Wind; for his people had besought him
greatly that he should quell the war of the winds, so that
the weather should regularly be hot or cold, wet or dry.
Tchamsem, the crafty, saw very well that he must needs
employ his wits rather than his weapons to deal with
these disorderly beings.

As he approached the house, the Master of the South
Wind caused a great smoke to go forth from the smoke-
hole; and the smoke blew in Tchamsem's eyes, so that he
was nearly blinded. The Master of the South Wind sat
with his back to the door, blowing the smoke out of the
smoke-hole. But Tchamsem brushed heavily against the
smoke-hole with his raven blanket, and the smoke puffed
back into the house and into the face of the Master of the
South Wind; whereupon the chief was seized with a
great fit of coughing. He left off blowing into the house
and came outside, still coughing and sneezing mightily,
to get a breath of fresh air.

"Ha, chief," cried Tchamsem, coming round to the
front of the house. "I wish you a very good day."

As soon as he could quit coughing, the chief replied:
"A good day! These are good days no longer, thanks to
that wretched brother of mine who calls himself North
Wind."

"Sit down, chief," said Tchamsem, in his most persua-
sive tones. "Perhaps I can tell you how to overcome this

unruly brother, so that you may have full dominion over him."

"Ah, my friend," returned the Master of the South Wind, "do but show me such a thing and I shall reward you greatly; so will my two brothers, who are much vexed at North Wind's antics."

"You have a daughter," counseled Tchamsem. "Both the sons of North Wind desire to marry her. Do you give her to one of the sons in marriage, and she will rule him even as every pretty woman rules her husband, and through him she will rule North Wind, her father-in-law. Moreover, the other son will be madly jealous of his brother and will set all his plans at naught. In this manner you will have dominion over North Wind, without recourse to any further storms or violence."

The Master of the South Wind was captivated by this

idea, and without delay he gave his consent to the marriage of his daughter to Icehead, son of Chief North Wind. And North Wind was overjoyed, for he fatuously fancied that in this way he would gain control over the Princess and her father; and, indeed, he was wearied of the unequal strife and was glad to have peace between the families.

Chief North Wind gave a great wedding-feast, to which all the different winds were invited and many of the far-flying birds. When the guests were all assembled, the Master of the South Wind brought the bride, his daughter, with strong winds and heavy rains. So Drops-of-Fresh-Water became the bride of Icehead.

After the celebration the Master of the South Wind went back from the north to his own country, carrying the heavy rains with him.

Drops-of-Fresh-Water had come to the house of her father-in-law too thinly clad, though wearing much heavier clothes than in the house of the South Wind. North Wind and his sons said it was an uncommonly warm season; but even so, when winter came on and the rivers and ponds were all frozen and the icy blasts blew from the north, the poor Princess was chilled to the bone. Her husband and her father-in-law went half-naked and complained of the unseasonably warm weather. They would have no fire in the house, it was so warm, they said. The daughter of the South Wind sat in the house all day, her teeth chattering, her lips blue with the cold. At times she wept softly, and was very miserable. When night came and she was in bed with her husband, who was well named Icehead, she was nearly frozen.

So the plan of ruling North Wind through his pretty daughter-in-law came to nothing.

(XXVII): Tchamsem Regulates the Seasons

One day the Princess went out and sat down on the beach. She was weeping bitterly, when she espied her father's old friend, Tchamsem.

"O Raven! Raven!" she cried. "Come and talk to me; I am so miserable!" And she told him her unhappy story.

When she had finished, Raven said to the Princess:

"Take this piece of yellow cedar-wood and carve it in the shape of a wedge." And she did so.

"Now take your salmon-knife," continued Tchamsem, "and make the wedge into the image of a duck." And she did as she was bidden, and the wedge became a little wooden duck, to the very life.

"And now," said Tchamsem, "tell the little wooden duck your troubles." Drops-of-Fresh-Water obeyed.

"Put the duck into the sea," Tchamsem commanded. This she did, saying: "Go to my father's country and tell my father, the Master of the South Wind, what is happening to me in this wretched place!" And instantly the duck came alive and swam southward.

And the duck came to the house of the South Wind, and told the Master of the South Wind all the troubles of the Princess, his daughter.

The chief was sitting with his chieftainess in front of his house when the duck arrived. And he and his wife were both very angry, so that the chief threw a stone at the duck before she had finished her story.

The duck dived, and the stone fell harmless. Then the duck came up again and said: "Since new moon your daughter has been cast out by her husband."

Again the chief threw a stone, and again the duck dived. The duck came up a second time and repeated: "Since new moon your daughter has been cast out into the storm by Icehead, her husband."

Then the Master of the South Wind stood up and said to the wild duck: "Go, tell my daughter that I am send-

PROUD RAIN WENT FORTH IN THE FACE OF THE
WIND, IN THE FORM OF A HUGE CLOUD.

ing her eldest brother." So the duck dived again and came up and swam fast and far and took the message to the Princess.

And the Master of the South Wind said to his eldest son:

"My son, go north and bring back your sister from the house of Icehead her husband."

And Proud Rain, the eldest son, went forth in the face of the wind, in the form of a huge cloud. But before he had gone half-way, the strong wind from the north began to blow hard, and his cloud was driven back. His sister wept when she saw her brother driven away.

Then the Master of the South Wind said to his second son:

"My son, go forth and bring back your sister!" And Scowling Face went northward.

Now the Princess saw her brother coming in the form of a black cloud. But he fared no better than the other; and when his sister saw him driven away, she cried more bitterly than before.

Chief South Wind said to his third son: "Go forth, my son Rain-Under-the-Knee!" and the third son went northward, in the form of hard rain. The Princess saw him coming, and she was glad; for she did not believe that the north wind could overcome him. But the cold breath of Chief North Wind turned the rain into sleet, and Rain-Under-the-Knee went back to his own country.

And his sister wept as if her heart would break.

Then the Master of the South Wind summoned his youngest son. And he said: "You are my youngest son, and my best-beloved son. But you are smaller than any of your brothers, so how can you hope to rescue your sister where they have failed?"

Whereat Going-Behind-Mountains, the youngest son, answered stoutly: "I am small, my father, but I have a brave heart and a crafty mind. I will go north and bring back my sister from the country of the North Wind." So he went forth—a very small cloud with a sharp edge.

On the way he met Tchamsem, who was flying about in his raven blanket.

"Keep behind the mountains," advised Tchamsem. "You are small, and you can pass between the high peaks."

So Going-Behind-Mountains went slowly northward, and he obeyed Tchamsem's advice. The north wind blew hard against him, but he kept the mountains between himself and the wind, and it could not drive him back. He stopped a little while until the fury of the wind had spent itself; then he went forward.

At length he came to the village of North Wind; and when the chief came out, the small warm cloud settled about his head, and the chief sank down and slept. Whereupon Going-Behind-Mountains tried to find his sister. But she was locked fast in her father-in-law's house, and her brother could not get in.

When the three elder brothers saw that the north wind had ceased to blow, they were very glad; and they hurried northward, with great clouds and with black storms and with heavy rain. So the ice was melted, and the house of North Wind was full of water; and the Princess sat on a cake of ice and floated round.

At last, when the ice was nearly all melted, Chief North Wind awoke and unlocked the door of his house, saying: "Go! take your sister and come no more to my country!"

But Icehead interposed and begged that he might have her six months out of the year. And the other brothers of Going-Behind-Mountains were jealous of his exploits. And they could not agree on anything.

So Going-Behind-Mountains said: "Let us call our friend Raven, and let him decide between us." And they all cried: "Yes, let us call Tchamsem!" And they sent for Tchamsem, and he came in his raven blanket, with the great crest of his clan.

And Tchamsem ruled that each of the winds should have three months—North Wind should have three months in winter, the Master of the South Wind three months in the fall, West Wind three months in summer, and East Wind three months in the spring.[1]

[1] This allocation of the winds is in accordance with the meteorology of the Northern Pacific coast.

He ruled also that the Princess, Drops-of-Fresh-Water, should spend only the three months of summer with her husband in the country of the North Wind, remaining the rest of the year with her father and mother and four brothers. And so the War of the Winds was brought to an end by Tchamsem, and the seasons were established.

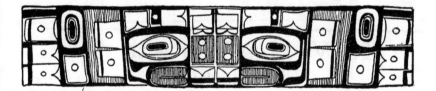

(XXVIII) : War with the Thunderbird

Now, in ancient times, of all the birds of the air, just as Raven was the craftiest, and Eagle the most voracious, the Thunderbird was by far the most terrible; at all seasons of the year men were afraid to go forth to gather berries or attend to their hunting, lest they be destroyed by the Thunderbird.

So it came to pass that Tchamsem was importuned by his people to make war on the Thunderbird and curb his rapacity.

But Tchamsem, however bold and daring, was nevertheless, above all things, cautious and exceeding crafty. Whereupon, on being requested to do battle, he first summoned a council of all the creatures that fly upon two wings, to deliberate as to just how the war was to be waged against Thunderbird.

To this council came Eagle, the insatiate, the undefeated in combat; and Pelican, whose wisdom antedates the world, being the gift of the high supernatural gods; and Woodpecker, that wise one in all the knowledge of trees and streams and in the secrets of the equinox; there came also Ngok, the Owl, whose knowledge of big medicine was unsurpassed; and Gull, the great trickster; and Wâax, the Bat; and Sawbill Duck Woman, half-sister of the Tide Woman; and many others.

So all the birds sat down and began to talk—all but Ngok, the Owl, who looked stupendously at nothing and kept his big thoughts to himself. And they made Tchamsem leader of the meeting; but he wisely said nothing until the others had spoken.

Eagle began the parley: "I will seize Thunderbird in my talons," he said. "I will bear him to my remote house on the rocks, and there will I rend him even as a young pigeon is rent, when my claws sink into his flesh."

Pelican said: "There are many ways to destroy the Thunderbird, but as yet none have been revealed by the high supernatural gods. Let us therefore rather apply ourselves to the crippling or curbing of his inordinate power." And they all perceived his words had wisdom.

Woodpecker drummed loudly, and the birds made an end of their chattering. "We cannot overcome Thunderbird by force of arms; perchance we may win by cleverly

wrought snare and device. Now, it happens that I know something of this creature's habits and limitations: how he is strongest in summer and weakest in mid winter; and I would counsel a well-reasoned attack in the wintertime, when his strength is abated by the cold blasts." There was a murmur of approval when Woodpecker left off speaking.

Ngok, the Owl, said nothing; but he looked as if what he knew would be well worth saying if he chose to speak.

Then said Gull, that inveterate gambler: "There is no god like the god of Chance. I will gamble with Thunderbird for his thunder; I will roll hoops with him. My great hoop is Rolling-Fog, and his hoop is Flash-of-

Lightning. We shall see then who is victor."

And they applauded this speech and voted that before declaring war they would send Gull to gamble with Thunderbird.

So Gull got his huge hoop, which men call Rolling-Fog, and went forth to Thunderbird's house and challenged him to come out quickly with his hoop, Flash-of-Lightning. And after so long a time Thunderbird put on his rainbow-feathered blanket and came out of his house.

"Aha!" he said, "old trickster! And so you have come at last to gamble with Thunderbird—with me, to whom lightning is but a toy, and the thunder a plaything! Aha, old trickster!"

But he brought forth his great hoop, Flash-of-Lightning, and prepared to gamble with Gull.

"And for what shall we gamble?" he asked. "For my part, I will stake the thunder. With what will you match it?"

"With my great hoop, Rolling-Fog," answered Gull.

"Wrinkles of my grandmother!" cried Thunderbird. "You have brass indeed, to propose such a thing! Fog against thunder? I demand something to boot, that we may gamble fairly."

"What do you ask?"

"You must put up your hoop, Rolling-Fog, and your wife as well. I will stake the thunder, and the odds will be fairly divided."

So Gull agreed; and he staked his hoop, Rolling-Fog, and his wife, Red-Winged-Flicker, who was counted the most beautiful of all the birds. And they gambled; not since the world began had there been such a terrible game.

First Gull sent forth his hoop, Rolling-Fog, and it blotted out the sunlight and loomed high in the mountains. Along the shore it sped, and the noise of it was like the sound of hard rain.

Then Thunderbird hurled his hoop, Flash-of-Lightning, and all the earth was lit up with the blaze. The other birds, who hovered about to watch the game, were nearly blinded. Only Ngok, the Owl, and Wâax, the Bat, stared unwinking; but that was because they were blind already. And the noise of the hoop was like a thunder-storm in late summer; it was heard even by the high supernatural gods, so that they stirred languidly in their seats and said: "A mouse is gnawing!"

After the hoops had gone more than half-way round the world, Flash-of-Lightning caught up with Rolling-Fog, and there was a loud crash, and a blaze as if all the heavens were afire. So Flash-of-Lightning broke through Rolling-Fog, and Gull's great hoop went to pieces in a tremendous shower of rain; and the laughter of Thunderbird was frightful beyond imagining.

Then Thunderbird came and claimed his prize, Red-

SO THUNDERBIRD LIFTED RED-WINGED-FLICKER
IN HIS TALONS AND BORE HER AWAY TO HIS OWN
COUNTRY.

Winged-Flicker, who was Gull's wife. But Gull refused to surrender his wife to Thunderbird, saying that the game was not played fairly.

Whereat Thunderbird laughed again. And he came once more to Gull's house, with much wind and lightning, and the wind and lightning drove through the house, and the roof was torn off. So Thunderbird lifted Red-Winged-Flicker in his talons and bore her away to his own country. Thus Gull at the same time lost his mighty hoop and his wife, whom he loved so dearly; great was his grief, and the anger of the other birds was kindled to avenge the wrong done to Gull's household.

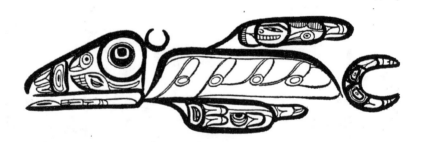

(XXIX): Tchamsem Overcomes the Thunderbird

Then Tchamsem came in his raven blanket and said to Gull:

"Fear not lest the theft of your dear wife go unavenged. I am Tchamsem, the Raven. You it was who helped me to get the herring for my people; and Raven does not forget easily."

And Gull was glad, and he published it abroad among all the birds and animals, saying:

153

"Come and hear what Tchamsem, the Raven, has to say about making war upon Thunderbird."

Wherefore they all came together in council, only more numerous than before, for now the animals were there, and they waited in silence to hear the words of Tchamsem.

"The Thunderbird must be snared in his own greed and rapacity," he said. And he unfolded his plan; whereat there was much rejoicing, for the birds approved of it mightily.

Tchamsem summoned Grouse, the great carpenter, and caused him to build a whale out of cedar-wood, very strongly put together and large enough to contain all the animals. Into the belly of this whale went Wolf, and Bear, and Dog, and even Mouse, and all the animals under heaven. In the stern of the whale sat Gull and Woodpecker and the other birds; but astride the whale's head, just behind the mouth, sat Tchamsem, and he steered the whale by pulling at its jaws—all of which was big medicine.

Now, about this time Little Pitch, that very rich man (who had never recovered from his experience with Tchamsem), fell sick and died. So Tchamsem—who, as you know, had a pledge against all his goods—fell heir to Little Pitch's body. At this Tchamsem was glad, for he had a wonderful plan; to wit: he smeared with pitch all over the outside of the wooden whale; and when the

ASTRIDE THE WHALE'S HEAD, JUST BEHIND THE
MOUTH, SAT TCHAMSEM, AND HE STEERED THE
WHALE BY PULLING AT ITS JAWS.

birds and animals wondered thereat, he shook his head wisely and said: "We shall see."

After so long a time the wooden whale went forth, with the animals inside, Tchamsem on the whale's head, and Woodpecker and the other birds in the stern. And they sailed many days, and at last they came to the coast of Thunderbird.

Out of his house came Thunderbird and his children; the noise of their wings was as a storm in summer. And the young birds perched on the wooden whale, ready to destroy the invaders as soon as they should come forth.

But the wings and legs of the young Thunderbirds were stuck fast to the pitch wherewith Tchamsem had smeared the outside of the wooden whale; try as they might, they could not free themselves.

Then Tchamsem hooted at Thunderbird, who came forth and prepared to launch his thunder against the whale, but he saw the whale covered with his own children. And Tchamsem caused the whale to dive, so that half of the young Thunderbirds were drowned. Had he caused the whale to stay under but a short time longer, they would all have perished.

Now when Thunderbird saw the plight of his children, and how they were stuck fast to the wooden whale, he called aloud to Tchamsem:

"Hoi! Hoi! Raven! Raven! Spare my children, and I will do what you ask."

So Tchamsem stood upon the whale's head, and he told Thunderbird that if he would return Red-Winged-Flicker to her husband and agree to keep to his own house in the winter and go forth in the summer months only, he would spare the young Thunderbirds that yet lived and take the wooden whale and the staunch fighters that it contained back to the Nass River country, whence they started. And the Thunderbird agreed, and Tchamsem caused Mouse to come out of the whale and gnaw the young birds loose, which he did without hurting them at all.

And Thunderbird gave a great feast, to which he invited Tchamsem and his companions. The feast lasted three moons, during which time they did not leave off eating and drinking.

Then Tchamsem and the birds and animals went back to their own country, all in the wooden whale, as they came. And that is why we have thunder in the summer: because of Tchamsem's victory over Thunderbird.

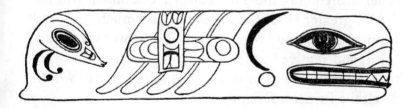

(XXX) : Tchamsem Returns to the Town of the Air

After overcoming the Thunderbird Tchamsem was indeed a greater chief than ever; he had much property —skins, copper, and many slaves. But he was yet dissatisfied, and resolved at length that he would try a third time to rediscover the country of Chief Echo, where dwelt the Princess Evening Sky.

So he set forth, alone and on foot; and whether it was months or years that he wandered he knew not;

THIS WAS THE TOWN OF THE AIR; AND THERE
WAS A CHILL AND LONELINESS ABOUT IT
WHICH OPPRESSED THE STRONGEST WITH A
HUGE HEAVINESS.

but one summer afternoon he found it, the Town of the Air.

The sun was dropping behind the houses, and they stood very black and still against the red glories of the west. A stray dog had wandered out of town, and fawned in front of Tchamsem, licking his feet. Tchamsem was about to kick the animal out of his path, but pity overcame him. The poor creature seemed famished and lean for want of food. Tchamsem stooped and patted it on the head, at which the dog gave a grateful bark. As he entered the town the animal followed him, emitting now and then a most dismal whine.

An unearthly stillness hung over the town—a stillness that was touchable and that played with one's hair as the damp breath of a cavern. The only sign of life was where here and there a wreath of smoke curled upward from the roof of the houses, crawling snake-like about three spans in air and then spreading out into a flat moveless cloud. In the whorls of this smoke Tchamsem fancied that he saw goblin shapes. They climbed silently upward, bending and twisting and mouthing for all the world like the river ghosts he himself had destroyed.

This was the Town of the Air; and there was a chill and loneliness about it which oppressed the strongest with a huge heaviness.

Tchamsem walked on through the deserted streets, his

heart beating as if it were in a great void; for it seemed as if he had been hollowed out inside, and he felt momentarily as if he would collapse, like a bag when emptied of its blubber. In front of him he soon noticed footprints. He saw that they stopped about five paces ahead. But as he walked, the footprints made themselves afresh in front of him. Even as he looked, the new prints would appear on the ground. He glanced over his shoulder, and, behold, there were other footprints following. These, too, appeared always about five paces behind. Then Tchamsem knew that he was surrounded by the people of the Town of the Air. He was preceded in front, and followed behind. But all the while he saw no living persons—only those mysterious footprints appearing on the moist ground as if of their own accord. When he stopped, the footprints stopped; when he went on, they went on. At last he could stand the suspense no longer. He turned and struck violently at his invisible pursuer. His medicine painted stick whistled through the air. It encountered nothing; but as it descended, it blazed forth with a greenish flame. And there was a sound as when the limb of a tree snaps asunder.

Tchamsem felt himself assailed from behind. Had not his raven blanket been drawn over his head, his skull would have crushed in like an egg-shell beneath the blow. He staggered forward, dazed; and as he did so, he stumbled over a body lying across his pathway. He fell headlong, and his magic stick escaped from his grasp and rolled out of his reach on the ground.

Before he could rise, he was seized by a dozen invisible hands. The air grew black as if a great blanket had been wrapped around the earth.

(XXXI) : Tchamsem and Evening Sky

When Tchamsem came to himself, he was lying in the same house he had entered before, where he had met the invisible Princess.

Again he felt the cool touch of viewless fingers, and a bowl of wine moved to his lips as of itself and he slaked his thirst.

"Lie still," whispered Evening Sky. "I will try to

manage your escape again. But it will be harder than before."

"It is not escape that I am looking for," replied Tchamsem. "Unless I can break this enchantment, I care not for life."

"You must value your life but little," said Evening Sky, "or you would have never come here again. Why did you do it, when you know it is certain death?"

"Because of you," replied Tchamsem. "Rather would I face certain death with the chance of obtaining you than life that is duller than death without you."

Evening Sky made no answer, but he felt the touch of her lips upon his forehead.

"Where is my painted stick?" pursued Tchamsem, at length. "If I had that, I should fear nothing; nay, but rather would I slay these devils and free you from this enchantment."

"Where did you have it last?" inquired the girl. "Perhaps I can find it for you."

Tchamsem described as best he could the place in which he had done battle with the invisible men.

"Trust me, and if there is aught in woman's wit," said Evening Sky, "you shall have your club again before nightfall."

"Have I lain here a whole day?"

"A night and a part of the day. Last evening it was that they brought you here; and my life is not worth two spiders if you escape again."

So saying, the Princess left him, and he lay there bound hand and foot, staring moodily into the fire.

The hours dragged by. At noon came Chief Echo, the invisible, swearing great oaths and demanding dinner. A pot was simmering on the fire, but no Princess was there to serve it. Tchamsem heard heavy footsteps in

front of him, and presently the pot got up off the fire and poured some of its contents into an earthen bowl. The chief ate from the bowl, muttering to himself, and swearing all the while. When he was done, the spoon dropped back into the bowl with no hand near it, and the footsteps went out again. After that there was more long waiting.

At length the door opened, and he knew by a sight

that was not with eyes, and a hearing that was not with ears, that it was the Princess. Before her, seemingly floating in the air, came the painted stick.

Tchamsem would have cried out for joy, but her hand was over his mouth in an instant.

"Here is your magic rod," said the Princess, "and assuredly it is big medicine; for with one blow of it you slew our strongest man, excepting only the chief, my father. Any other weapon in the world would have passed through him harmlessly. Now, for the love that you bear me, do this: take this weapon and fight your way out of this town, nor ever come hither again."

"That I will not do," replied Tchamsem, "for if I left the Town of the Air without freeing you from your enchantment and bearing you off with me in safety, the gods themselves would mock me as a coward, and I should be more miserable than the taboo people in the bottom of the sea."

"Why do you talk thus when if you stay here to watch for one more sun, you will meet certain death? Then I, too, would destroy myself, that I might join you in another world."

Tchamsem was silent at this, and his heart was exceedingly sad. At last he held aloft the alder rod which had been dipped three times in the spring with a piece of moon in it, and painted thrice with the blood of the stars. Joyfully he held it aloft.

"Now will I try the virtue of this greatest medicine," he said, in a voice so loud that Evening Sky put her hand over his mouth again: but it was too late, for almost immediately the door opened, and Tchamsem knew that he was discovered. His arm dropped with a downward swing, and as it did so, the alder rod touched the invisible Princess, and she flashed into view; the enchantment dissolved and she stood forth clearly. But meanwhile he saw very dimly the bloodless larvæ of his assailants closing in upon him. His alder rod in his right hand, he advanced to meet them for a last combat.

At this moment he heard the voice of the Princess; it rang loud and clear.

"Let them alone!" she cried. "They are too many for you! Strike that elk's head with your painted rod!"

Now any other man than Tchamsem would have thought that this was nonsense and would have fought the invisible folk, wherein he would have erred, for invisible people were coming in great numbers, and they would have worsted him.

But, heeding the words of the Princess, Tchamsem sprang lightly aside and touched the elk's head with his painted rod of alder. As he did so, there was a flash as of lightning, and four thunders rolled from the four quarters of the heavens. Three times the lightning flashed, and the four thunders rolled in and rolled back again. The town, the invisible folk, the whole enchantment, vanished; and Tchamsem and the girl found themselves standing alone in an open place whereon there was neither tree nor stone.

And there was a great potlatch and giving of copper and elkskin and red beads when Tchamsem and Evening Sky returned to the big village of his people on Nass River. And even to this day it is common among all the Tshimshian folk to say of a beautiful woman: "She is as fair as Evening Sky, the bride of Tchamsem."

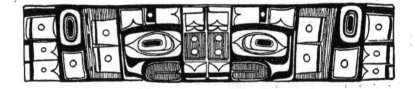

(XXXII): The Last Adventure of Tchamsem

So Tchamsem, hero of eleven exploits, of which stealing the daylight was the first and getting married to Evening Sky the eleventh, lived long and happily with his wife and children in the midst of his own people and was a great chief. And many years passed, the number of which you would not believe, for in those days folks lived to an astonishing age; and as for Tchamsem, was he not the grandson of the Oversky Chief? And was he not also Raven himself, whom the high supernatural gods had blessed with dateless winters?

But Tchamsem was minded to do yet one more mighty deed. For he wearied of ease and plenty, and he bethought him of one exploit that had not been done.

Time out of mind, Gûlhak the Crab, that monster of the sea, had visited the shore every so often, and each time he devoured one hundred souls. Men and women alike he destroyed and even young children; none escaped. They might survive many years, but their fate was certain; he got them all. (Backwards he went, after he had eaten his fill of human beings; that is why he was called Gûlhak, which means "He Who Walks Backwards.")

Now, the place to which Gûlhak went was at the bottom of a profound whirlpool and was called Living Depths Horror. There the Howhow dwelt, that giant devilfish who always fought with Gûlhak the Crab, so that Gûlhak gave up his hundred souls that he had swallowed; and what happened then no man was able to tell, for none had returned after being caught by Gûlhak the Crab.

So Tchamsem left large stores of food and property, with instructions for their disposal if he should fail to get back, and kissed his wife most tenderly and set forth to meet his last enemy. About him was his raven blanket, very black and glossy; and he carried his magic club, which was big medicine.

For many days he walked along the shore, but saw nothing of Gûlhak the Crab. At length he sought the advice of Logobolâ, that very wise shaman, who lives in a cave overlooking the sea and is said to hold communion with the high supernatural gods.

"Why do you wish to find Gûlhak?" asked Logobolâ. "Do you not know that the Crab has another name? The high supernatural gods have named him Death."

"Though he had fifty names," Tchamsem replied, "yet would I seek him, for I have tasted of all the dangers of heaven and earth save the danger of Gûlhak the Crab; and I am minded to try this last adventure."

"Well do you speak of it as your last adventure," responded Logobolâ. "For so it has been unto all who have encountered Gûlhak: none have returned, and even I, the wisest of the shamans, wot not what is become of them."

"Nevertheless, I would try my wit and prowess against the Crab," said Tchamsem.

So Logobolâ instructed him as to the place where he would be likeliest to meet Gûlhak the Crab, after the backward-walking one had had his fill of human beings and was retreating to the sea.

Tchamsem spread his raven blanket and flew swiftly to the spot described by the great shaman—a place lonely

and desolate beyond imagining, where the rocks overlooked a gray, pebbly beach, and where the sun never
shone, because of the mist that always rolled in from the
whirlpool. Tremendous was the noise, as the breakers
ripped and tore along the shingles; and Tchamsem fancied that he could hear the roar of the whirlpool itself
above all the tumult.

How long he waited he never knew; for the days and
nights were barely distinguishable. Tchamsem was
aware only of a gnawing hunger, and a faintness that
grew steadily upon him, as his legs became more and
more numb with the cold.

At last he perceived a huge, slowly crawling object,
the same color as the rocks, making its way across the
beach. Its clumsy legs and claws moved with a sort of
blind jerk, for the creature was going backwards.

It was Gûlhak the Crab.

Tchamsem spread his raven blanket and flew down
from the cliff and alighted gently on the Crab's great,
horny back.

The Crab could not feel Tchamsem on his back, for
his shell was very thick. And Raven made himself very
light, so that the creature was not aware of the added
burden.

So they came nearer and nearer to the surf, and at
length the Crab quickened his pace and began to back
steadily into the cold, snarling brine. And Tchamsem

INTO THE SEA PLUNGED GŪLHAK, WITH TCHAM-
SEM CLINGING TO HIM.

lay flat on the Crab's back and grasped the edge of the shell firmly with his two hands, lest he be washed away.

Into the sea plunged Gûlhak, with Tchamsem clinging to him; and the water was indeed deathly cold. Tchamsem felt a singing in his ears, and everything was black; and his heart swelled up in his breast until it seemed surely that it would burst.

(XXXIII) : Mouth at Each End

Tchamsem never knew how he reached the bottom of the whirlpool. But he knew that when he opened his eyes, he felt for the first time the icy breath of Fear. Then he understood why the whirlpool was called Living Depths Horror.

On the slimy rock floor coiled and uncoiled the tentacles of the Giant Devilfish. His great greenish unwinking eyes, protruding terribly, looked up with a malevolent stare. Silent, and with sickening slowness, the two creatures edged towards each other, ready to begin their combat.

Tchamsem thought desperately and fast. The Crab, now plainly conscious that he was burdened with some foreign object, was reaching back nervously with his claws. But Tchamsem's greatest danger was from the tentacles of the Howhow. Quickly he leaped from the Crab's back and planted himself on the Devilfish's dome-like head. The real fight had begun.

Gûlhak the Crab struck out with his claws, and the Howhow tried to snare his adversary with his hundred tentacles. Tchamsem clung to the monster's head, protecting himself as best he could with his raven blanket. At length it was plain that the Crab was beginning to tire. His eight legs and two claws were no match for the hundred arms of the Giant Devilfish. And as his movements grew slower and it seemed that a sort of poison entered him whenever one of those terrible fingers touched an unguarded spot, he began disgorging one by one the victims he had swallowed, and the Howhow seized each in one of his tentacles. So it was, until the hundred souls which Gûlhak the Crab had devoured were in the grasp of the Devilfish's hundred arms. All this Tchamsem saw from his vantage point on the monster's head. And he saw the Crab retire, backward as was his habit, edging his way up out of the whirlpool.

In each of the tentacles of the Howhow was a human

being, white and naked. Tchamsem knew by their writhings that they still lived—if such a thing could be said—but whether they cried aloud or were silent he knew not, for the roar of the whirlpool choked every other sound.

Some were strong men, in the prime of lustihood. Some were graybeards. Beautiful girls there were, and old women, bony as witches. He beheld also infants and a few children, their small shapes barely visible in the clutch of those tentacles.

Now, as Tchamsem watched these naked people in the clutches of the Howhow, a strange thing happened. The monster squeezed them all to the same size—dwarfs not larger than the smallest infants. And the Devilfish began moving, with his living burden, to what seemed to be a mouth of black water in the middle of the rocky floor; and, reaching it, he oozed in, bearing his hundred human souls. And had not Tchamsem been protected by the raven blanket (which was big medicine), he must assuredly have perished in the rush of icy water as they fell, and rose, and fell again—clean through the thick bed-rock whereon dark-faced Amalah stands and holds the pole of the world on his chest; so far they fell that they came to the *other mouth* and could fall no longer. For the black hole is called Mouth at Each End; it has no bottom; it is perfectly straight, yet at whichever end you start down, you will come up out of the other.

So the Giant Devilfish climbed out of Mouth at Each

End, holding the hundred little figures that had once been people, and with Tchamsem still clinging to his head. And, behold, they were in the Oversky Country!

Raven looked, and he saw clearly the house of the Oversky Chief, and the high hill whereto he was wont to take the box of daylight. And he fancied that he saw the shambling forms of the three slaves, Old-Man-Who-Foresees-Trouble, Big-Sounding-Drumbelly, and He-Who-Knows-Everything-That-Happens. But of Princess Moon and her father and mother he as yet saw nothing.

Now for the first time the Howhow spoke, and Raven crouched low upon the monster's head and listened.

"You have chosen to follow the way of mortals to their natural end, which is but a beginning. I remain but a short while in this country; then I go back through Mouth at Each End to meet the Crab. Will you now begin all over again as Raven in the Oversky Country, and will you carry these souls to earth and implant them in the bodies that Elderberry shall create, and will you return and get the daylight, and so on as before? Or will you rather reverse the story for the time being and return with me as we came, through Mouth at Each End? Answer me quickly."

And Tchamsem, mindful of his wife and children at home, and of his slaves and property, chose to return as he had come.

Whereat the Howhow buried in the caves of the Over-sky Country the human souls that he had brought, await-ing the next visit of Raven.

"For you will come again," he said. "Through Mouth at Each End you will come; and next time you will re-main. And it will be a beginning, a new beginning, for you and for the world. It is the will of the high super-natural gods."

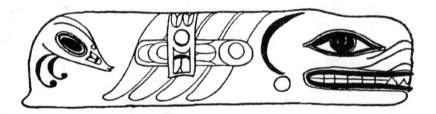

Printed in the USA
CPSIA information can be obtained
at www.ICGtesting.com
CBHW071210240524
9052CB00014B/1152